Collection Management: Preparing Today's Bibliographers for Tomorrow's Libraries

Collection Management: Preparing Today's Bibliographers for Tomorrow's Libraries has been co-published simultaneously as *Journal of Library Administration*, Volume 28, Number 2 1999.

Collection Management: Preparing Today's Bibliographers for Tomorrow's Libraries

Karen Rupp-Serrano, MLS, MPA
Editor

Collection Management: Preparing Today's Bibliographers for Tomorrow's Libraries has been co-published simultaneously as *Journal of Library Administration,* Volume 28, Number 2 1999.

Routledge
Taylor & Francis Group
New York   London

Collection Management: Preparing Today's Bibliographers for Tomorrow's Libraries has been co-published simultaneously as *Journal of Library Administration,* Volume 28, Number 2 1999.

© 1999 by The Haworth Press, Inc. All rights reserved. No part of this work may be reproduced or utilized in any form or by any means, electronic or mechanical, including photocopying, microfilm and recording, or by any information storage and retrieval system, without permission in writing from the publisher.

The development, preparation, and publication of this work has been undertaken with great care. However, the publisher, employees, editors, and agents of The Haworth Press and all imprints of The Haworth Press, Inc., including The Haworth Medical Press® and The Pharmaceutical Products Press®, are not responsible for any errors contained herein or for consequences that may ensue from use of materials or information contained in this work. Opinions expressed by the author(s) are not necessarily those of The Haworth Press, Inc.

First published by

The Haworth Press, Inc., 10 Alice Street, Binghamton, NY 13904-1580 USA

This edition published 2013 by Routledge

Routledge	Routledge
Taylor & Francis Group	Taylor & Francis Group
711 Third Avenue	2 Park Square, Milton Park
New York, NY 10017	Abingdon, Oxon OX14 4RN

Routledge is an imprint of the Taylor & Francis Group, an informa business

Cover design by Thomas J. Mayshock Jr.

Library of Congress Cataloging-in-Publication Data

Collection management : preparing today's bibliographers for tomorrow's libraries / Karen Rupp-Serrano, editor.
     p. cm.
     "Co-published simultaneously as Journal of library administration, volume 28, no. 2, 1999."
     Includes bibliographical references and index.
     ISBN 0-7890-1002-X (alk. paper)–ISBN 0-7890-1003-8 (pbk : alk. paper)
     1. Academic libraries–Collection development–United States. I. Rupp-Serrano, Karen.
Z675.U5 C64247 2000
025.2'1877–dc21   00-021761

Collection Management: Preparing Today's Bibliographers for Tomorrow's Libraries

CONTENTS

ABOUT THE EDITOR

Karen Rupp-Serrano is Social Sciences Librarian and Associate Professor of Bibliography at the University of Oklahoma Libraries. She holds an MLS from Emporia State University and an MPA from the University of Oklahoma.

Preface

As a subject bibliographer, I have had concerns about several collection development issues throughout my career. Cooperative collection development, locally available data, managing personnel at varying career stages, vendors, selecting the right mix of resources, and serials collection management have all presented continuing challenges to me over the years. Discussing these issues with colleagues, I found I was not alone in my concerns.

As I talked with other and heard their thoughts, it occurred to me that there was a need to address some of these topics in a more concrete manner than over a coffee cup. This compilation is a result of that decision. I have called upon professionals from a variety of backgrounds with a wealth of expertise, asking them to speak to these issues, providing practical advice and stimulating further thought.

Authors from several backgrounds address seven different issues in this work. Adrian Alexander, of the Big 12 Plus Library Consortium, discussed cooperative collection development among libraries and explores its potential in an increasingly automated environment. Molly Murphy and I address interlibrary loan and document delivery data and its applicability to collection development decision making. Dana Alessi of Baker and Taylor speaks to vendor service trends for today and tomorrow.

Susan Fales of Brigham Young looks at the skills needed by those who supervise bibliographers, from assessing electronic resources to balancing the needs of librarians at different points in their career paths. Gay Dannelly of Ohio State provides an overview of the networked environment and recommends how to best achieve a balance of resources within it. Leslie Haas of the University of Utah explores the wealth of local data librarians should consider as they make collection development decisions. Julie Hurd scrutinizes the issue of responsible serials management on limited resources. My thanks go out to all of these people for their willingness to address these issues; I believe they have provided us with much food for thought.

© 1999 by The Haworth Press, Inc. All rights reserved.

It is my hope that other collection development professionals will read this work and find it of use. It is written with both the novice and experienced professional in mind, and is designed to address some of those vexing questions that librarianship continually faces.

Karen Rupp-Serrano

Toward "The Perfection of Work": Library Consortia in the Digital Age

Adrian W. Alexander

SUMMARY. The decade of the 1890s was a watershed period for library cooperation in America. A century later, another milestone has been reached as new consortia are created primarily for the purpose of providing cost-effective access to electronic resources. This paper provides a brief history of library cooperation in America, with emphasis on the latter half of the 20th century. Motives for library cooperation, along with potential obstacles and keys to success are identified, and a nexus between service quality improvement and library cooperation is noted. The role of library consortia in the current electronic environment is described, with particular emphasis on the 1990s, during which the Internet has matured and became widely available. Finally, prospects for the future of library consortia are outlined, with a description of key environmental factors that will affect them. *[Article copies available for a fee from The Haworth Document Delivery Service: 1-800-342-9678. E-mail address: getinfo@haworthpressinc.com <Website: http://www.haworthpressinc.com>]*

KEYWORDS. Library consortia, library history, International Coalition of Library Consortia

The close of the decade of the 1990s is an appropriate juncture at which to examine the burgeoning phenomenon of interlibrary cooperative efforts. In his landmark paper on the history of cooperative programs among academic libraries, Weber noted in 1976 that "the

Adrian W. Alexander is Executive Director of the Big 12 Plus Libraries Consortium, Linda Hall Library, 5109 Cherry St., Kansas City, MO 64110. He holds an MLS and a Certificate of Advanced Study in Library Administration from the University of North Texas. He is active in the LITA and ALCTS divisions of ALA as well as the International Coalition of Library Consortia (ICOLC).

© 1999 by The Haworth Press, Inc. All rights reserved.

decade of the 1890s witnessed the beginnings of major national programs of academic library cooperation."[1] A hundred or so years later,
we have reached another important milestone in library cooperative
activities. Hirshon believes that "we will remember the 1990s as the
decade when organizations made the final leap from the industrial age
to the service and information age."[2] To be sure, it has been a pivotal
decade in terms of the proliferation of network-based electronic resources (indexing and abstracting databases, full-text journals, etc.)
that have become a major focus of our current cooperative efforts. It
also has been a decade that not only has seen new library consortia
created and organized all over the world but also has seen many of
those consortia organize themselves into an increasingly influential
federation of library cooperatives. And it all started with cataloging.

A BRIEF HISTORY

The history of library cooperation is as long as the history of "professional" librarianship in America. In 1876, the new American Library Association created a Committee on Cooperation in Indexing
and Cataloguing College Libraries, consisting of the librarians of the
University of Rochester, Cornell University, Vassar College, Syracuse
University, and the New York State Library. This committee presented
a report in 1877 which called upon academic libraries "to speak out on
any special adaptation of the cooperative cataloging movement which
was required for their special wants," since this work was being done
at that point principally in the public libraries.[3] The report then em-
barked on a path that could be considered a portent of things to come
in both cataloging and cooperative efforts by proclaiming that "the
first most important thing to be aimed at is perfection of work."[4]

The concept of shared cataloging began in earnest during that pivotal decade of the 1890s when the American Library Association began
publishing analytic cards as part of a shared indexing/cataloging program in January 1898. This project was later taken over by the H. W.
Wilson Company as part of the International Index of Periodicals. At
about the same time, interlibrary lending emerged as a focal point of
library cooperation. The librarian of the University of California announced in 1898 that he would be willing to lend books from his
library to those that would reciprocate. A year later, the librarian of
Princeton University proposed "a lending library for libraries" and

named the Library of Congress as a logical candidate for this important role. A few years later, in 1907, the Library of Congress issued a policy governing interlibrary loans and by 1909 had lent over 1,000 volumes to 119 libraries, including 49 academic libraries that accounted for over half of the loans.[5] During the same period, notes Kopp, an article appeared in *Public Libraries* (1905) titled "Universal Library: A Plea for Placing Any Desired Book within the Reach of Any Person Wishing to Make Reasonable Use of Same."[6]

In his 1976 article, Weber included union catalogs in his list of cooperative activities although he was not entirely sure whether these important projects qualified as such.[7] The first regional union catalog dates to 1901 at the California State Library and covered both periodicals and nonfiction books. The National Union Catalog began a year earlier and began selling both printed catalog cards and their galley proofs in 1901. The early part of the century also marked the genesis of the first cooperative acquisitions programs, beginning with a South American "expedition" in 1913-14 organized by Northwestern University. While thousands of books, newspapers, and manuscripts were acquired for Northwestern's library as well as others, that university's chief librarian, Walter Lichtenstein, was not entirely satisfied with how the program fared, particularly regarding the process for making purchases for more than one library: "The chief difficulty was that the material could not be readily divided until my own return to this country, with the result that no one knew until I did return how much each institution was liable, and hence I was considerably hampered in making further purchases. . . . When the collections came to be divided it was soon felt that the only possible way to divide the cost among institutions interested was to devise a system of points. A pamphlet was counted as one point, an unbound volume as four, and a bound volume as eight."[8]

Ironically, the next watershed event in the history of library cooperation in the U.S. may have been the Great Depression, according to Weber, because "there was impetus for cooperation which led to new programs . . . " Weber cites evidence of "dozens of new union card catalogs begun in the 1930s and notes that a 1940-41 ALA survey of these programs recommended future coordination "to assure thorough coverage, minimum overlap, and sound fiscal support."[9] Other new cooperative activities during the 1930s included the Cooperative Cataloging Program, which began in 1932 and included almost 400 U.S.

and Canadian libraries within a decade. On a smaller scale, several regional arrangements, both formal and informal, began during this decade. Weber specifically cites the Cooperating Libraries of Upper New York (CLUNY), formed in 1931 and including seven libraries, and a 1931 formal agreement between Duke and the University of North Carolina which was expanded in 1955 to include two other North Carolina institutions. The Joint University Libraries was founded in 1936 and included Vanderbilt, George Peabody College, and Scarritt College for Christian Workers, and was formed as a jointly owned and financed independent entity with its own board of trustees. In 1933, the Atlanta University Center Corporation was formed with a grant from the State of Georgia for the purpose of reciprocal borrowing among the libraries of Atlanta University, Morehouse College, Spelman College, Morris Brown College, and Clark University. Finally, this decade marked the first example, in 1932, of the "unification of academic libraries under state control" by the Oregon State Board of Higher Education. The board appointed one director of libraries for the entire university system and established programs for reciprocal borrowing and central ordering.[10]

As with many other 20th century social phenomena in America, the end of World War II was the next significant event in the development of library cooperative programs. The growth of higher education and the flourishing of scientific research which followed the war provided a unique opportunity for developing, as Weber asserts, programs that were "more formal, more extensive, and far more expensive than previous efforts."[11] Examples of post-war programs include the Universal Serial and Book Exchange, Inc. (USBE) in 1948, the beginning of the Farmington Plan (1948) for cooperative foreign acquisitions, the initial formation of what eventually became the Center for Research Libraries (1951), and the Latin American Cooperative Acquisitions Program (1959).

By the end of the 1960s, regional and statewide consortia were not an unusual occurrence, by any means. In her monumental 1972 study, Patrick identified over 125 consortia that were just focused on academic libraries and were formed from 1931 and 1971. Of these, over 90 percent had been founded since 1961.[12] Patrick observed that economic pressures and an expanding universe of information (this was almost 30 years ago) were creating "pressure toward consortium development" and forcing academic libraries "to rely more and more on access, through reciprocal arrangements, to the specialized collections of companion libraries."[13] The other major development during this time that contributed to the growth of the consortium phenomenon was, as noted by Kopp, the introduction of computer processing into library operations and the emergence of shared bibliographic data-bases.[14]

Kopp also believes that other developments "overshadowed" consortia in the 1970s and 1980s. Specifically, he mentions the growth of what he calls "megaconsortia," also known as bibliographic utilities. Kopp cogently observes that the activities of member-driven utilities such as OCLC, the Research Libraries Group (RLG) and the Washington Library Network (WLN) "were direct outgrowths of those activities for which library consortia had been formed up through the early 1970s. With the rise of these services, there was somewhat less of a need for some interlibrary cooperation among groups of libraries."[15] This became especially true during the late 1980s and into the current decade as the "megaconsortia" began to expand their service offerings beyond their traditional shared cataloging and interlibrary loan activities. This, in turn, prompted regional networks such as AMIGOS, BCR, and SOLINET, to name a few, to begin diversifying their service offerings as well. Now, these organizations compete, in effect, with more local library consortia in some areas of interlibrary cooperation. Shared access to a number of electronic databases is probably the most evident example of this phenomenon in today's consortial environment.

MOTIVES, CAVEATS AND KEYS TO SUCCESS

America's libraries have a rich history of cooperative programs involving libraries of all types and in all parts of the country. Most of these programs have been successful to a degree, with some more so than others, while other programs have been less than successful. There appear to be a number of factors that can contribute to the success or failure of library consortia, as many, perhaps, as there are reasons for creating them in the first place. Simpson identifies three primary reasons why libraries participate in cooperative programs. The first is to "enhance the quality of services that a library provides to its clientele."[16] Allen and Hirshon agree, noting a connection between a growing emphasis in library management in the 1990s on quality improvement and renewed interest in library consortia. This connection between quality and consortia works in two ways: (1) consortia members can share information about and thus foster the development of best practices, and (2) they can reduce the "unit cost of providing core services."[17]

Simpson's second reason for library cooperation is what he describes as the "altruistic" nature of the library profession: "sharing is good and working together seems to be the professionally right thing to do."[18] This sentiment may be, in one sense, what Weber alluded to when he observed that "the challenges, the opportunities, and the problems do not seem to change fundamentally with the passing of time."[19] From the very beginning of librarianship as a profession in America, we have been looking for both reasons and opportunities to cooperate, almost by second nature, Simpson seems to be saying.

Simpson's third reason is that "librarians strongly believe in resource sharing as a means to reduce libraries' costs."[20] Reed-Scott also identifies cost sharing/reduction as a principal objective, at least for resource sharing or cooperative collection development programs, but ties this objective closely to that of increasing "timely access to materials [that] users need and that are not available in local collections." These two premises, she believes, "have undergirded resource sharing programs for more than half a century."[21] In examining the role of publicly-supported academic libraries in particular, Eaton sees a similar link. A typical goal for such libraries organized in regional or statewide consortia is to "pool their resources to contain costs and maximize access for their constituencies."[22] Potter notes in this regard that academic libraries, in particular, have "long-formed consortia for the purpose of sharing existing physical resources . . . in recognition of the fact that a group of libraries has a combined set of resources that is greater than the resources of a single member."[23]

Writing 25 years ago, McDonald identified a total of nine different reasons why libraries cooperate: financial constriction, cost sharing, availability of funds, pressure from numbers, resource improvement, service improvement, management improvement, image enhancement, and technological development. A more concise list is that of Becker—service, economics, and technology,[24] but McDonald also pointed out some obstacles to success that may still hold true today: "a persistent attitude that assigns cooperative activities low priority and low or no budget"; and an assertion "that cooperation causes delay and inconvenience resulting in a general deterioration in service."[25] The problem of budgetary constraints on cooperative activities is changing, especially at the state level, as new statewide programs, funded directly by the respective legislatures, have emerged in the 1990s in Texas, Georgia, Virginia, and elsewhere. Indeed, as Kopp points out, a "receptiveness to public-private collaboration has aided in the resurgence or creation of some consortia. Political entities and funding sources have been more supportive in recent years of these types of library cooperation."[26]

The "excuse" cited by McDonald regarding delay, inconvenience and deterioration of service is a difficult one to "prove," especially since there still remains in librarianship a distinct lack of management tools for measuring the quality of library services. Another way to describe this obstacle, however, is in the context of the need to give first priority to local constituencies. In this sense, it probably always has been an obstacle and always will be. In many ways, the words of Ernest Colwell (a university president), written in 1952, are as true today as they were almost 50 years ago:

> ". . . the obstacles to co-operation are not material. . . . [They] are found in the mind and spirit of man. They are institutional pride and institutional jealousy. . . . They are inertia and complacency. . . . And I would say, finally, that it is an irrational provincialism or an emotional particularism on the part of college faculties which makes co-operation difficult."[27]

To overcome universal and substantive obstacles such as these requires a great deal of those engaged in collaborative work. In a recent and outstanding article on academic library consortia, Allen and Hirshon identify several factors that are essential to the success of library cooperatives. "Above all else," they note, "[the consortium's] members must have a high degree of respect for, and deep-seated recognition of, the value of increased collaboration." I would add that this value must be intrinsic in every member of the group, because as Allen and Hirshon point out, "this becomes more critical as a consortium grows larger." A willingness to "compromise individual institutional goals to help advance the common good" is also important, and goes to the heart of Colwell's observation about institutional pride and institutional jealousy.[28]

A third key is "constant support throughout all levels of the organization." A collaborative atmosphere must be developed and encouraged that permeates each member library, because directors by themselves cannot make a consortium successful. All staff who may have a direct role in cooperative programs "must receive support to make the partnership successful, and be encouraged to generate a result greater than what any individual institution could do on its own." Finally, Allen and Hirshon point out, library directors and consortium leaders "must not be afraid to take risks, to commit resources, and to encourage action. . . . "[29] To develop this kind of collaborative organizational dynamic, it is essential that the consortium develop a comprehensive and well-articulated strategic plan early on. Such a plan must have both active participation and/or political "buy-in" from the member libraries' directors, and must be shared and discussed with all library staff members to insure understanding and acceptance.

CONSORTIA AND THE ELECTRONIC ENVIRONMENT

Libraries have organized cooperative projects around automated systems and information technology for almost 40 years now, but the 1990s may prove to be the decade in which these efforts reached a new and exciting level of richness, complexity, and importance. This milestone can be linked directly to the maturation and ubiquity of the Internet in the early part of the decade, followed soon afterward by the availability of graphical browsers and the World Wide Web. Quickly, libraries found themselves presented with intriguing new opportunities to provide access to a rapidly growing array of full-text electronic content with rich graphics and jazzy hyperlinks to cited references, formulae, datasets, etc., all in a distributed network environment. The "virtual library" actually had arrived.

These exciting developments were part of what Kopp has described as "the confluence of several technological, fiscal, organizational, political, and other dynamics in the late 1980s and early 1990s" that "created an environment well suited for what many consider a 'resurgence' of library consortia." Libraries were achieving at this time, says Kopp, "certain levels of local systems and networking sophistication" but were also faced with skyrocketing costs for print resources, especially serials. Meanwhile, libraries and many of their parent organizations were being either "down-sized" or "right-sized" and policymakers and administrators were encouraging more collaboration and cooperation, in the never-ending quest to do more with less.[30]

So, while library consortia had been active and prolific for many years, the new networked electronic environment has provided them with new opportunities and challenges. As publishers and other providers of electronic content rushed to develop new products for the library market, libraries soon learned that the price tag for many of these new products was sometimes very high; in some cases, in fact, it was prohibitively high for a single library. Library leaders were quick to see the opportunity for sharing costs for these products either by means of existing consortia, some of which may not have been very active of late, or had previously been focused on other activities, such as the regional bibliographic networks; or, they simply began forming new consortia. As Potter observed in 1997, "libraries are forming alliances for the purpose of identifying and addressing common needs arising from developments in information technology, especially the growing importance of the Internet and the World Wide Web."[31]

Publishers of electronic content were not enthusiastic, initially, about the prospect of the marketplace forming increasing numbers of "buying clubs" directed toward their products. It became apparent to most, however, that library leaders were serious about this move, especially after the formation in 1997 of the loose federation that was known initially as the "Consortium of Consortia" and was re-named the International Coalition of Library Consortia (ICOLC) in 1998. This powerful market force, now comprising 102 separate cooperative groups in the United States, Canada, Europe, Israel, and Australia, has become, as Allen and Hirshon describe it, "a reverse cartel because these independent consortia come together not to limit competition or fix prices, but to leverage their collective power to open up the market."[32] The semi-annual meetings of the ICOLC feature presentations by invited publishers and vendors that are interested in working with library consortia and which have developed consortial pricing for their products. In early 1998, a presentation by representatives of Congressional Information Services (CIS) at an ICOLC meeting, and a subsequent meeting with members of an ICOLC task force, led directly to a revision by CIS of its pricing structure for its Academic Universe product.

In March 1998, a number of ICOLC member consortia adopted a "Statement of Current Perspective and Preferred Practices for the

Selection and Purchase of Electronic Information" that was drafted by several key ICOLC leaders. This document "sets forth concerns about the current electronic information environment, the desired environment for the future, and the preferred practices for library consortia and their member libraries to achieve the desired outcomes." Its intent is to "define the current conditions and preferred practices for pricing and delivering scholarly information within this emerging electronic environment." Finally, the statement "aims to provide a starting point for a dialog among information providers and library consortia." The document goes on to identify and discuss in detail a list of "Current Problems and Needs for the Future" (increasing expectations vs. stable budgets, fair use, archiving, the current scholarly communication system, pricing strategies, measures of effectiveness), and "Preferred Practices in the Emerging Electronic Information Environment" (contract negotiations, pricing, access, archiving, licenses, management data, authentication).[33] Similar statements on other aspects of the electronic information environment have been adopted or are being drafted. Topics include guidelines for statistical measures related to Web-based resources and technical issues in contract negotiations.

In 1995, Jutta Reed-Scott wrote of resource sharing in research libraries that "The most transforming factor is the rapid emergence and development of electronic information technologies that make it possible to envision different ways of organizing collections and services that libraries have traditionally provided."[34] Apart from the electronic content issues already discussed, library consortia are working with these technologies in other exciting ways as well. The linking of member libraries' online catalogs is becoming an increasingly popular topic, especially with improvements being made to the Z39.50 standard. A leader in this area is the Committee for Institutional Cooperation (CIC), which consists of thirteen academic research libraries in the Midwest. The CIC's "Virtual Electronic Library" will provide access to all CIC library OPACs via a common, Web-based front-end. The local systems will be able to authenticate any CIC borrower's ID and "validate the loan from another library to the borrower without staff intervention."[35] Similarly, any electronic resources jointly licensed by the CIC members, as well as digital libraries created locally or collectively within the CIC, will be accessible via the same Web interface.

It is difficult to assess the degree of success that library cooperatives have experienced at this point with regard to the emerging electronic information environment. As Kraus observed in 1975, the "literature of library cooperation is very large, and most of the articles are uncritical . . . there are few evaluative reports that give a clear account of the success of a venture and the factors leading to success or failure."[36] Certainly, the professional literature has improved in this regard since then, but in the case of today's electronic environment, it is still too early to assess the results accurately or comprehensively. The anecdotal evidence suggests that this is a highly successful area for library cooperation, if on no other basis at this point than the sheer popularity of it. Certainly, the ICOLC has played a major role in this regard, providing a focal point for library consortia to work together as a true "mega-consortium." In only two years, its numbers have grown considerably and it has assumed a pre-eminent position of leadership in the profession in terms of defining the issues and outlining the collective needs of the marketplace. This achievement alone will come to be regarded, in all probability, as one of the greatest in the history of library cooperation.

PROSPECTS FOR THE FUTURE

Allen and Hirshon begin their study of the current state of academic library consortia by stating that "the most important development for academic libraries during the current decade has been the move from organizational self-sufficiency to a collaborative survival mode as personified by the growth of library consortia."[37] The concept of a "collaborative survival mode" is an important one to keep in mind when considering the future of library consortia, because two important "environmental" factors will continue to pose a challenge to libraries as we move inexorably toward a new decade, a new century, and a new millenium. The first factor is that of budgetary constraints that have been a fact of life for libraries for many years, and there is no reason to assume that the situation will change any time soon. As Eaton observed of academic libraries in 1995: "There is no indication that the financial picture will reverse itself, given the economic pressures facing higher education in general."[38] In this case, libraries will be compelled to continue with cooperative programs for the forseeable future.

The other factor is one which, when combined with that of budgetary constraints, has created one of those classic "between a rock and a hard place" scenarios. Simply put, the cost of information, especially scholarly information, will continue to increase at a rate that many libraries will find difficult to match with budget increases. At the same time, the amount of information that is available will continue to increase, presenting continuing collection development challenges for libraries. This "two-headed" dragon of rising prices and more information was spawned, in effect, by a long-standing system of scholarly communication and publishing that needs to change, but will not do so in a substantive and systemic way in the near future. Cooperative collection development, therefore, has become more important than ever before and provides an essential program opportunity for many library consortia.

Technology will continue to be the other major area of opportunity for library cooperatives. As Hirshon points out, "information technology has become so assimilated into our operations, but so expensive to maintain, that it must be used as effectively as possible."[39] From bibliographic utilities to shared integrated systems to local and networked online databases, library consortia have a long and successful history of applying information technology in a collaborative way to provide more services while sharing the cost. According to Allen and Hirson, "consortium directors envision an important role in leading and coordinating the adoption of new and emerging technologies to enhance member library services."[40] While we will probably never achieve the "perfection of work" goal envisioned in 1877, the track record that library cooperatives have established in information technology, and other programs as well, provides every reason to expect a bright and productive future.

NOTES

1. Weber, David C. "A Century of Cooperative Programs Among Academic Libraries." *College & Research Libraries* 38:206 (May 1976).
2. Hirshon, Arnold. "Library Strategic Alliances and the Digital Library in the 1990s: The OhioLINK Experience." *Journal of Academic Librarianship* 21:383 (September 1995).
3. Weber, 206.
4. "Cooperative College Cataloging." *American Library Journal* 1:436 (August 1877).

5. Weber, 206.

6. Kopp, James J. "Library Consortia and Information Technology: The Past, the Present, the Promise." *Information Technology and Libraries* 17:8 (March 1998).

7. Weber, 207.

8. Lichtenstein, Walter. "Report to the President of Northwestern University on the Results of a Trip to South America." i 16:8-9 (September 1915).

9. Weber, 208.

10. Ibid.

11. Ibid., 212.

12. Patrick, Ruth J. *Guidelines for Library Cooperation: Development of Academic Library Consortia* (Santa Monica, Calif.: System Development Corporation, 1972): 2.

13. Ibid., 3-4.

14. Kopp, 8.

15. Ibid., 11.

16. Simpson, Donald B. "Library Consortia and Access to Information: Costs and Cost Justification." *Journal of Library Administration* 12: 86 (1990).

17. Allen, Barbara McFadden and Hirshon, Arnold. "Hanging Together to Avoid Hanging Separately: Opportunities for Academic Libraries and Consortia." *Information Technology and Libraries* 18: 37 (March 1998).

18. Simpson, 87.

19. Weber, 213.

20. Simpson, 87.

21. Reed-Scott, Jutta. "Future of Resource Sharing in Research Libraries." *Journal of Library Administration* 21: 67 (1995).

22. Eaton, Nancy. "Resource Sharing: The Public University Library's Imperative." *Journal of Library Administration* 21: 27 (1995).

23. Potter, William Gray. "Recent Trends in Statewide Academic Library Consortia." *Library Trends* 45:416 (Winter 1997).

24. Becker, Joseph. "Information Network Prospects in the United States." *Library Trends* 17:311 (January 1969).

25. McDonald, John P. "Interlibrary Cooperation in the United States," in *Issues in Library Administration,* Warren M. Tsuneishi, Thomas R. Buckman and Yukihisa Suzuki, Eds. (New York: Columbia University Press, 1974): 131.

26. Kopp, 11.

27. Collwell, Ernest C. "Inter-Library Cooperation." *Library Quarterly* 22:2-3 (January 1952).

28. Allen and Hirshon, 43.

29. Ibid.

30. Kopp, 11.

31. Potter, 417.

32. Allen and Hirshon, 40.

33. http://www.library.yale.edu/consortia/statement.html

34. Reed-Scott, 68.

35. Shaughnessy, Thomas W. "Resource Sharing and the End of Innocence." *Journal of Library Administration* 20(3):12 (1994).

36. Kraus, Joe W. "Prologue to Library Cooperation." *Library Trends* 24:171 (October 1975).

37. Allen and Hirshon, 36.

38. Eaton, 31.

39. Hirshon, 384.

40. Allen and Hirshon, 42.

Interlibrary Loan and Document Delivery: Lessons to Be Learned

Molly Murphy
Karen Rupp-Serrano

SUMMARY. Interlibrary loan and document delivery services have the potential to provide a wealth of information for collection development librarians. Insights into book and serial needs, departmental emphases, instructional opportunities and distant students are available from interlibrary loan and document delivery databases, provided librarians are willing to seek such information out and effectively utilize it. *[Article copies available for a fee from The Haworth Document Delivery Service: 1-800-342-9678. E-mail address: getinfo@haworthpressinc.com <Website: http://www.haworthpressinc.com>]*

KEYWORDS. Interlibrary loan, document delivery, collection development, distance education, interlibrary loan–statistics, serials management, remote access

In the history of library services, interlibrary loan and document delivery are fairly young. As such, they may often be given short shrift by more-established areas of the library world, such as cataloging or reference. But they are important services and they can have a great deal of impact on other areas of the library; they can especially provide relevant information to collection developers, enhancing their ability to provide needed resources to library patrons. It is the purpose of this article to address the potential of interlibrary loan and document delivery services and data to collection development.

Molly Murphy is Document Delivery Librarian for the University of Oklahoma Libraries.

Karen Rupp-Serrano is Social Sciences Librarianand Associate Professor of Bibliography at the University of Oklahoma Libraries.

© 1999 by The Haworth Press, Inc. All rights reserved.

LITERATURE REVIEW

It has only been in the past few decades that librarians have begun to systematically delve into an analysis of interlibrary loan and document delivery data and services, with an eye toward how they may best enhance library collection development activities. Much of this effort has been inspired by the development of spreadsheet, database and statistical software that make such analysis less time- and staff-intensive. A look at the past decade reveals several efforts inspired by the proliferation of microcomputers and database management software on which we have come to depend. It is imperative that we make the best use of this technology to tackle collection development questions and challenges. The proper use of interlibrary loan statistics can lead to a better use of the finances available.

In 1989, Laura Bartolo examined interlibrary loan/collection development studies to identify elements of interlibrary loan records having import for collection development and to determine how analysis of such can be extracted from interlibrary loan data for subject selectors.[1] In 1990, Williams and Hubbard described the development and use of a dBase III Plus database of interlibrary borrowing information to assist in making collection management decisions regarding periodicals.[2] Shortly thereafter Jo Ann Lahmon described efforts at the University of Tennessee in Knoxville to provide collection development selectors with relevant interlibrary information on a monthly basis.[3] This consisted of using WordPerfect to load and sort OCLC records, as well as generating reports from SAVE-IT sorted by the requestor's university department. Scott Mellendorf also reported on the applicability of SAVE-IT interlibrary loan data to collection development in 1993.[4] More recently, George Washington University's Gelman Library began using ISM's Aviso software to gather serial title data in support of selection efforts.[5]

There have also been several explorations of the implications of interlibrary loan and document delivery for collection development in the same time period. In 1993, Mounir Khalil urged that serial and monographic purchase decisions be based on a systematic analysis of collection use.[6] Khalil called for interlibrary loan statistics to be part of such an analysis, used to monitor collection strengths and weaknesses, highlight areas in need of inventory or replacement projects, and track curriculum and research pattern changes. In 1996, Syring and Wolf directed the conversation toward document delivery, urging collection developers to consider taking a portion of the budget "off the top" to fund document delivery services and to view such services as an integral part of collection development efforts.[7]

Graham Cornish urged that interlibrary loan be viewed "as an essential adjunct to collection management" in 1997, and explored the implications of newer document forms incorporating sound, moving images, computer software and interactive media.[8] He noted how the sale conditions or licenses of such documents usually limit a library's ability to meet interlibrary or document supply arrangements, thus forcing libraries to expand their electronic collections, often at the cost of more traditional paper collections. He also touched on document delivery services, pointing out their often limited selection of documents and their tendency to focus on areas where the money is, such as science, law, and engineering. Most recently, Etschmaier and Bustion looked at the evolving relations between document delivery and collection development.[9] They discussed the services provided by commercial document deliverers and their ability to enhance collections versus disadvantages such as inadequate coverage, poor vendor responsiveness and turnaround time. They touched on full-text, CD-ROM and online databases and their impact on interlibrary units and collection development budgets. Finally, they explored the implications of the profit incentive of commercial document suppliers on libraries, such as needing to maintain subscriptions to "unprofitable" titles, the impact of keeping such on monographic budgets, and the cancellation of serials to provide for document delivery services.

CURRENT TRENDS

Clio is one of the newest interlibrary loan management software systems to come on the market. Clio is a management system that keeps track of interlibrary loan transactions from the first time a patron makes a request throughout the entire life of the request. It includes overdue, billing, invoicing, archiving and statistical functions to ease the paperwork burden of interlibrary loan. The University of Oklahoma Libraries has been using the software since October of 1997. At this time, however, the full capability of the Clio reports has not been utilized by interlibrary loan or collection development.

There is a trade-off with such systems: in order for libraries to best utilize the wealth of data offered by software such as Clio, interlibrary loan staff must diligently maintain the database. It is not enough to trust that all the information being gathered is going to be correct and useful–frequent checking and updating must be practiced to ensure that it is the case for the database. A minor effort performed daily can make the statistics more meaningful and useful to all interested parties.

The most obvious information provided to collection development librarians by interlibrary loan and document delivery services is that of who requests what. By analyzing what book titles are being requested a librarian may, first of all, identify any titles which are repeatedly requested and note them for purchase; they are clearly a need unmet by the collection, and their purchase is nearly always less expensive than repeated requests via interlibrary loan.

Analysis of books requested also helps a collection development librarian determine trends in a discipline, thus allowing her to maintain currency. Not only is she kept aware of current trends, she can use this knowledge to direct her purchases, building the collection and providing better service to library patrons. Yet another piece of interlibrary loan data of use would be sudden changes in requests from a department. Such changes might indicate shifts in personnel or curriculum which warrant attention and increased liaison activities to a department.

To save time, some of this information could be automatically flagged for action. Titles requested more than once could automatically generate an order for purchase. Requests for titles from the current publication year could also be flagged for automatic purchase, as most lending libraries do not like to loan current materials. If liaison activities indicated that a department is making curriculum changes, supporting titles might be automatically purchased (requests from selected departments having key words or phrases could be identified with standard query language software). With such programs in place, a collection development librarian's time is saved, and in the case of new materials, items are identified and purchased quickly, before they go out of print. And of course, the user is better served, as the materials they need become available to them in the collection.

Such a program is in place at the University of Oklahoma Libraries. In 1994, library policy began to allow the absorption of interlibrary loan charges. This, in turn, allowed the creation of a procedure for the Libraries to purchase new or heavily requested titles on a "rush for

ILL" basis. However, the procedure was very labor-intensive and extensively involved both acquisitions and interlibrary loan personnel. Now that Clio software is in place, the ability to accomplish the same thing with much less effort is within reach.

Another application of interlibrary loan data involves usage patterns. Efficient use of the information available to collection development librarians from ILL management databases would enable them to address questions from their departments about specific interlibrary loan service usage patterns of their faculty and graduate students. For example, Clio can generate a collection development report for books consisting of patron department, short title, number of transactions per patron (for that title), author, imprint and date fields. A collection development report for copies consists of patron department, short title, ISSN, and transactions per patron. The main drawback to this format is inconsistency; patrons don't always enter their names or departments in the same way, and as a result the information is not as useful.

SERIAL DECISIONS

Arguably, even more valuable information regarding serials is available from interlibrary loan and document delivery services. Titles which are heavily requested from such are obvious candidates for subscription, as often it is less expensive to maintain a subscription and/or purchase older volumes than to make continual requests for such materials which may result in the added cost of copyright fees. Individual issues which are heavily requested may lend themselves to an automatic purchase program as well; such titles are often special issues of a journal devoted to a particular topic, and including them in the collection meets user needs while simultaneously easing the burden of interlibrary loan staff.

A number of libraries have utilized serials information to make such decisions, as demonstrated in the literature review. Beginning in October of 1996, the University of Oklahoma Libraries started an Uncover pilot project which attempted to determine the ownership versus access issue for specific titles. As part of the project, the Libraries identified ninety journal titles from the chemical and engineering sciences whose subscription costs totaled more than two thousand dollars per year. In addition to continued access to the titles in paper format, unmediated document delivery from Uncover was allowed for those departments' faculty and graduate students for the identified titles. Over the course of two years, there were no cases where the cost of unmediated document delivery exceeded the cost of the subscription. It has not yet been decided by the Libraries, however, if this is a realistic way to determine what serial subscriptions will be cut.

One may also use document delivery data to determine potential serial title cancellations. By allowing patrons to request articles from journals to which one also has a paper subscription, data may be collected on the use of those titles. Titles rarely requested via such services may perhaps be canceled, and the occasional need for them more economically met via document delivery. Naturally, this depends a great deal upon their subscription cost.

On a more anecdotal level, continued requests for materials that are in the library's collection may point to still other needs. It may be that a particular individual may be in need of specialized instruction to help them better utilize the library. Sometimes the same may be true of a department, indicating a need for increased liaison activities or library instruction.

Today serials data grow ever more important, due to the increased number of full-text and citation databases. This is an area where interlibrary loan/document delivery librarians and collection development librarians truly must work together very closely. Careful analysis and thought have to go into subscription decisions for full-text databases. Overlap with the collection is one consideration in such decisions. Coverage is another. Unfortunately, coverage is often such that collection overlap must be maintained. That is, often coverage of a title is limited in some way, most often in that only certain document types are available full-text, such as reviews or letters, or that the current year is not available full-text, thus pointing to a continued need for a library subscription.

CHANGING HABITS

How often should interlibrary loan statistics be shared with collection development librarians? With superior database management software in place, these reports can be generated and dispersed to interested librarians on a monthly basis, at least. Document delivery suppliers such as UMI and Uncover usually provide the ability to generate monthly statistics on usage. Uncover statistics, for example, can track the number of times a journal title has been ordered, who ordered it, what department that patron comes from, the cost of the article, etc.

This data feeds back into the serial decision-making loop. In such instances, a good economic indicator is to compare the total cost of items ordered from one journal to the subscription cost of the title. The University of Oklahoma Libraries' Uncover pilot project was an effort to do just that. And while pressures from outside the library's decision making process must be considered in such decisions, they should not be the ultimate factor in determining additions or cancellations to the library's collection. Rather, collection development librarians can use statistical information gathered from these reports to "prove" use or disuse of certain sections of the library's collection by certain academic departments.

Do interlibrary loan departments typically share their statistics with collection development? An informal query to library consortia, as well as subscribers to the interlibrary loan listserve, elicits a wide range of responses–from no sharing of information at all to the inclusion of the interlibrary loan librarian in collection development meetings and purchase decisions.[10] Some libraries have what could be described as a formal cooperative effort between ILL and collection development, in which ILL generates reports on a regular basis (monthly, quarterly, or annually) and shares them with subject librarians. Collection librarians then base some purchasing decisions on information gathered in this way. Some libraries report that the statistical spreadsheets themselves are saved onto a LAN so that all librarians can access and use the reports as they wish. Such reports can consist of lists of journal titles ordered (typically the copyright compliance report), and lists of books ordered by patrons, usually broken down by departments or call number. Some reports may include author, year of publication, patron status and number of times a specific title has been requested. Query respondents who have more information included in their reports (call numbers, request numbers, article titles, departments and patron status) state that they have more formal cooperative efforts in place and share information at specified intervals. Some of the less formal methods of information gathering reported consist of collection developers querying the interlibrary loan librarians about what subject areas they think need more purchases. Some ILL librarians make suggestions about book purchases and some are responsible for choosing items for direct purchase rather than attempting to obtain the item via ILL. One described keeping a "mental note" of subject areas ripe for purchasing.

DISTANT STUDENTS

Another area where interlibrary loan/document delivery data grow in importance is in regard to services to distant students. Often the most common contact between distant students and the library is the service provided by interlibrary loan and document delivery departments. And these services are heavily impacted by collection development decisions: which monographs and journals a library has to loan to distant students, and which remote databases are available to them, are decided in great part by collection development librarians. In turn, data about materials which are requested by such students should be available to collection development librarians. Just because a student is not on campus, that does not mean that the collection should not be developed to meet their needs as well, no matter their location.

Distant students should be treated as a category of their own as well as a select group of users from whatever discipline of which they are a member. Distant students rely on the interlibrary loan department for their library services and represent a unique category of patrons for statistical study and analysis. They are requesting items from the library's collection for the majority of their library needs but also require some things the ILL department has to obtain for them. Their use of the library's collection can and should be studied by collection development librarians in order to better understand library usage patterns. Items distant students request from outside the collection (about one-third of their total items requested) should also be studied to determine areas lacking in the library's collection–just as any other user groups' usage should be studied. The advantage to using statistics generated by distant students is that there is no guessing involved. Collection development librarians can analyze everything a group of distant students has asked for to determine what, if any, areas of the collection are lacking (or are particularly useful).

CONCLUSION

The 1993 National Interlibrary Code states that "Interlibrary borrowing is an integral element of collection development for all libraries, not an ancillary option," a statement that also applies to document delivery and only grows more true with each passing year and each new service wrinkle.[11] Precious dollars must be wisely spent, and interlibrary loan and document delivery data is a wealth of information available to collection development librarians to help them make sound purchase decisions. Collection development librarians should be cultivating such data, using it to better serve patrons and themselves.

The "ideal system" as defined by Shirley Baker and Mary Jackson in 1992 does not yet exist.[12] Admittedly, the "current systems" in place in 1992 have for the most part been updated to include many of the features they found lacking. New systems are capable of load leveling, delivering collection development data, easing the burden of paper invoicing, and eliminating paper files.

Baker and Jackson's definition of the ideal system included the patron's unsuccessful search of the home catalog, which in turn would prompt the system to search a bibliographic utility. From there, the request could be made simply and easily to the lending libraries normally chosen by interlibrary loan staff. The newly introduced ClioRequest (the newest Clio product), in conjunction with OCLC's Direct Request, gives us hope that we are closer to unmediated interlibrary loan than ever before. However, even when that ideal system exists, it will be useless unless cooperation between interlibrary loan and collection development is in place. The system must generate monthly (at least) reports of books and serials requested in interlibrary loan, and collection development must exhibit a genuine interest in, and active use of, these reports. Interlibrary loan must benefit from sharing the information, either by recognition and thanks from the library administration, or from seeing actual purchases of books and serial titles which then become part of the collection.

Improvements to existing interlibrary loan management software systems continue. Developers of the various softwares are usually very receptive to suggestions from the users: Larry Perkins, CLIO developer, encourages subscribers to the CLIO listserve to add to a Clio "wish list" at any time. All suggestions are considered, and many are implemented in upgrades. Suggestions to OCLC personnel also are often considered when making improvements to many of OCLC's products and services. Interlibrary loan librarians working with collection development librarians are best suited to decide what changes are necessary to existing software and should regularly ask for and expect those improvements to make their borrowing and purchasing decisions more fruitful.

NOTES

1. Laura M. Bartolo, "Automated ILL Analysis and Collection Development: A Hi-Tech Marriage of Convenience," *Library Acquisitions: Practice and Theory* 13 (1989):361-369.

2. Brian W. Williams and Joan G. Hubbard, "Collection Management Uses of an Interlibrary Loan Database," in *The Best for the Patron: Proceedings of the MPLA Academic Library Section Research Forum,* eds. Randall J. Olson and Blaine H. Hall (Emporia, KS: Emporia State University, 1990):31-49.

3. Jo Ann Lahmon, "Using Interlibrary Loan Data in Collection Development," *OCLC Micro* 7, no. 5 (1991):19-22.

4. Scott A. Mellendorf, "A Practical Method for Using Interlibrary Loan Data to Assist Librarians with Collection Development," *OCLC Systems and Services* 9, no. 2 (1993):45-48.

5. Gale Etschmaier and Marifran Bustion, "Document Delivery and Collection Development: Evolving Relationship," *The Serials Librarian* 3, no. 3 (1997):13-27.

6. Mounir A. Khalil, "Applications of an Automated ILL Statistical Analysis as a Collection Development Tool," *Journal of Interlibrary Loan, Document Delivery and Information Supply* 3, no. 1 (1993):45-54.

7. Millie L. Syring and Milton Wolf, "Collection Development and Document Delivery: Budgeting for Access," in *Advances in Collection Development and Resource Management,* Vol. 2, ed. Thomas Leonhardt (Greenwich, CT: JAI Press, 1996):49-62.

8. Graham P. Cornish, "Electronic Document Delivery Services and Their Impact on Collection Management," in *Collection Management for the 21st Century,* eds. G.E. Gorman and Ruth H. Miller (Westport, CT: Greenwood Press, 1997): 159-172.

9. Etschmaier and Bustion, 22-26.

10. Big 12 Plus Libraries Consortium collection development librarians, conversation with the authors, 4 March 1999; Barbara McFadden Allen, CIC Center for Library Initiatives, conversation with the authors, 4 March 1999; Interlibrary Loan Listserve, March 1999.

11. "National Interlibrary Loan Code," *RQ* 20 (1980): 29.

12. Shirley K. Baker and Mary E. Jackson, "Maximizing Access, Minimizing Cost: A First Step Toward the Information Access Future," *Public Library Quarterly* 13, no. 3 (1993):3-20.

Raising the Bar:
Book Vendors and the New Realities of Service

Dana L. Alessi

SUMMARY. Library book vendors are facing new realities as we move toward the 21st century. Changes in continuations, firm order placement, value-added services, approval plans, retrospective collection development, and database creation and maintenance are being effected in an effort to keep current customers and attract new ones. This article addresses those changes and the subsequent shift to information-based vendors. *[Article copies available for a fee from The Haworth Document Delivery Service: 1-800-342-9678. E-mail address: getinfo@haworthpressinc.com <Website: http://www.haworthpressinc.com>]*

KEYWORDS. Book vendors, collection deveopment–business aspects, approval plans, retrospective collection development

As the new millennium approaches, traditional library book vendors are finding that they must reinvent themselves to meet the new realities of a business model for the 21st century and the changing acquisitions and collection development requirements of the academic library. Those that realize that they are now in the business of providing information will survive and prosper; those that persist in clinging to the old archetype of merely providing monographs are doomed to failure.

The model of the academic library book vendor until the early 1990's had been to provide firm order service to libraries, supplying

---

Dana L. Alessi is Director of Sales and Marketing for Academic Libraries for Baker & Taylor.

© 1999 by The Haworth Press, Inc. All rights reserved.

the orders which libraries sent, reporting on items which could not be supplied with standard reports such as Not Yet Published, Out of Stock, Out of Print, etc, and supplying titles as they arrived from publishers, no matter how long that might take. The standard of 30 percent supply in 30 days, 60 percent in 60 days, and 90 percent in 90 days was widely accepted, by both libraries and suppliers. For most of the academic vendors, inventories were limited to university presses, scientific and technical publishers, and selected academic publishers. Most vendors also offered Continuations or standing order services, for annuals or ongoing titles in series, and a core of vendors also offered Approval program services.

Although the majority of vendors supplied value-added services such as cataloging, processing, and pre-binding, most libraries did not avail themselves of these services, preferring instead to use their own staffs for copy cataloging, original cataloging, repetitive processing chores (often performed by student labor), and even binding services. Many of the vendors' cataloging and processing services offered only certain standard cataloging and processing options, which may or may not have fit with a library's local practices.

Even though libraries often had integrated library systems, including an acquisitions module, most orders received at vendors were still received the old-fashioned way–through the mail, on paper forms, either the traditional 3×5 or on a standard $8\ 1/2 \times 11$ sheet, and were reentered by massive order entry staffs. In the 1980s, several vendors began to offer more automated mechanisms of ordering and connecting directly to the vendor. Baker & Taylor developed the Bataphone, a hand-held device into which ISBNs could be entered and transmitted via telephone lines; Baker & Taylor, Blackwell, and Brodart also led the development of vendor personal computer based systems, which offered rudimentary electronic transmission to the vendor from the library.

If a library chose to place its Continuations with a library book vendor rather than a serials vendor, it usually employed the traditional ordering mechanisms of paper orders or lists. Often libraries simply checked off titles in vendor-produced catalogs and submitted the appropriate pages. Continuations Departments were extremely paper intensive in communication from library to vendor and vendor to library.

Approval services, developed in the early 1970s, also changed little from the established model. Libraries constructed profiles, maintained by the vendor, relied upon vendors for highly ball-park cost estimates, and could never really figure out what exactly it was that they could expect to arrive on their approval plans–or when. Approval plans were highly paper intensive, with 3 × 5 bibliographic slips placed in the books, and many more 3 × 5 bibliographic slips sent for notification purposes only. Both libraries and vendors were awash in a sea of slips.

When librarians had additional money for development of the collection to support new academic programs, or extra funds which had to be spent in a limited amount of time, they turned to standard bibliographies, stored publisher catalogs, or other in-house tools to identify possible titles. They sometimes chose neither wisely nor well. A few vendors did offer some rudimentary selection lists based on approval titles, but these reflected merely the original bibliographic information regarding the titles, and did not update in terms of publication status or price.

With the explosion of the Internet in the 1990s, the business model for vendors and the expectations of libraries began to change dramatically as new electronic models developed. What, then, are the new realities as we move towards the 21st century?

CONTINUATIONS SERVICES

Surprisingly, one of the most predictable services has been the last to change its fundamental practices. Continuations services still largely remain the same as they always have–labor and paper intensive. Although some vendors have been able to produce bibliographies and selection lists, and although at least one vendor offers an announcement service for new standing orders, there have been few innovations in standing order services. Indeed, serials vendors provide highly sophisticated automated services, but monographic vendors have lagged behind in development. Libraries using monographic vendors for Continuations by and large place orders the way they always have–through lists, paper orders, and some e-mail. Although vendors may respond to e-mail claims by return e-mail, extensive bibliographic information and status of titles is not as readily accessible as it is for monographs.

However, this model is changing. Baker & Taylor was saddled with an outdated 1970s-era Continuations system which was still reliant on microfiche to identify bibliographic information for titles and which did not comply with Y2K. Facing imminent crash of the entire Continuations system, Baker & Taylor decided in early 1998 upon a rapid development project to create an Internet-based interactive Continuations database and launched a prototype in summer 1998 at the American Library Association Annual Conference. The product, Compass, was thoroughly developed and tested with a Library Advisory Board comprised of academic and public library customers, and was activated for customer use in October, 1998.

With Compass, a library can identify titles to order, search for status information, check its current holdings, place orders electronically, and claim electronically, all via the World Wide Web. The Continuations database, consisting of over 40,000 titles, is searchable by keyword, title, publisher, ISSN, unique B & T series ID, and subject. Each title listing contains full bibliographic information as well as frequency, last issue supplied, next issue expected, and pertinent status information, such as whether the title has changed its name, continues another series, or has ceased. For more recent additions to the database, even fuller information is given such as an annotation, Tables of Contents, or even a scan of a jacket cover. For the first time, a library can make a truly intelligent decision regarding expenditure of precious standing order dollars. For example, a library developing a collection in business and desiring to enhance its Continuations in this subject can search on Business as a subject term, identify titles it does not already own, determine pricing, both current and historical, and even get into the meat of books through Tables of Contents to insure that the titles ordered will be truly appropriate to the collection.

Compass is designed to be flexible, user-friendly, and quick. Orders placed are confirmed as received the next day, and claims response is dramatically improved. For the internal Customer Service employees at Baker & Taylor, lives have radically changed. Because of Compass, customer service personnel are able to be more proactive and respond more quickly to customer orders and claims.

Through development of Compass, there has also been a dramatic change in service levels to customers. Timeliness of receipt of Continuations titles has significantly improved as Continuations has been mainstreamed into Baker & Taylor's regular Sales Order Processing System instead of being ordered, picked, invoiced, and shipped via a separate workstream.

The net results for customers are improved order handling, both at the library and internally at the vendor, less paperwork, greater efficiency, and speedier service. Other vendors have developed, or are in the process of developing, similar Web-based systems. These systems promise to make the traditional book vendor an even more viable source for Continuations services.

With these enhancements in services have also come increased pricing pressures for Continuations vendors. Continuations services are labor intensive, requiring an enormous amount of bibliographic research, monitoring, and claiming, far more than the routine monograph order. However, as libraries are evaluating their standing order processes and are comparing these to their mainstream monographic processes, they have increasingly pressured Continuations vendors for greater discounts, and most vendors have complied. We are now seeing Continuations discounts rising anywhere from 3 to 5 percent over prior levels from monographic vendors.

Libraries utilizing Continuations services, especially those where funds are stretched, are seeking other service enhancements, notably cycling, or the ability to receive a title on a regularly scheduled basis, but less frequently than the normal frequency of the title. For example, a library may opt to receive an annual directory, where little information changes from year to year, on an every two years or every three years cycle.

Other Continuations service enhancements offered by a variety of vendors include fund accounting, account transfers, and automated systems records interfaces and value-added services such as cataloging and processing.

Clearly, there are new models–and higher expectations for service–for libraries and their monographic Continuations vendors. For the many competing Continuations vendors, the bar has been raised in terms of service provision, and the bar must be met in order to remain competitive.

FIRM ORDERS

The bar has also been raised in the provision of the mainstream firm order. There are new realities for monographic vendors, and new service expectations from libraries. An already hotly contested firm order environment has become ever more contentious, with vendors rushing to provide the services which libraries now require to provide optimum service to their own clientele. No longer is it enough for the vendor to receive the paper firm order, provide routine status reports, supply the book in a reasonable amount of time, and ship the book with a paper invoice. The service requirements of today's libraries are far more sophisticated, and the competitive vendor must meet all of them in order to remain truly viable. Briefly, let us review these new service realities.

In 1990, Baker & Taylor received approximately 35 percent of its academic library orders electronically, through the Bataphone and the original PC-based system, B & T Link, which allowed libraries the opportunity to dial access the Baker & Taylor mainframe and transmit orders. Fax receipt of orders was non-existent, and telephone orders were used only for titles a library wished to rush. For other vendors with similar electronic systems, the percentage was consistent. Compare that with today's environment, where the paper order sent by "snail mail" has virtually disappeared. In 1999, Baker & Taylor receives over 65 percent of all academic orders electronically through a variety of ordering mechanisms, including the aforementioned B & T Link, e-mail, vendor systems, and the Internet. All electronic orders are routinely confirmed, with confirmations immediately sent to the library indicating not only that has the order been received and processed, but also the expected shipping status of the book–in stock, backordered, or out-of-stock, out-of-print, not yet published, Apply Direct, or otherwise unavailable from the publisher.

Additionally, telephone and fax orders have also increased significantly. Telephone orders are no longer confined to the occasional Rush order. Many libraries, especially corporate and smaller academic libraries, have found that the telephone order provides them a quick, efficient ordering mechanism, as well as instantaneous knowledge about order status, as confirmations of shipping status are given in each order session.

For libraries still confined to a paper environment, the fax machine has been able to shorten order turnaround by at least a week. Although orders must still be keyed into the vendor order system by order entry staff, faxing orders eliminates the usual mail delay of up to five days. Since a library is able to dial a toll-free number, faxing also saves the library postage and stationery costs. All faxes are also routinely confirmed in the same way that telephone and electronic orders are handled. Indeed, it is only the paper order which leaves a library to wonder exactly how long it will be before it receives a book. The paper order now is no more than 15-20 percent of all orders received, and the percentage is shrinking annually. Perhaps in another ten years, we will see the disappearance of the paper order entirely.

With a preponderance of libraries now utilizing integrated library systems, vendors have found that the traditional library/vendor relationship has altered to that of a triumvirate, with the ILS vendor now an integral part of the service equation. Not only must the library vendor support its own system, whether it is e-mail, personal computer, or Internet based, but it also must support the protocols of the systems vendor. For the book vendor, this now means that its systems staff must support BISAC, the original book industry standard, the newer X-12 standard, and now EDIFACT. Each ILS vendor has its own way of doing things, each its own quirks, and each its own timetable. It is sometimes difficult for the library to understand the delicate balance among these competing standards and competing systems, and that what may be priority for both the library and the vendor may not be priority for the systems vendor. Or that the book vendor may also have an array of automation projects of which working with a specific system is just one of the many.

Academic libraries also have increased expectations about timely receipt of a book. Never has turnaround time been so important to the library. As previously mentioned, the old standard of academic service was 30 percent of the order filled in 30 days, 60 percent in 60 days, and 90 percent in 90 days, with all titles supplied or reported by the end of 120 days. However, it was not at all uncommon for libraries to have a one-year cancellation date for standard domestic monographs, with the expectation that many titles were difficult to acquire from publishers. It may be the influence of approval plans and their timeliness of receipt; it may be the influence of our "hurry-up" society, but today the "just-in-time" mentality has considerably raised the bar on speed of supply.

Although academic libraries have not gone to the extent of the retail store model, cascading their orders to vendors to get full effect of inventory, they are now, more than ever, changing their expectations of service. The new service expectations are 60 percent in 30 days, 90 percent in 60 days, and full completion of an order in 90 days.

Those vendors who have an extensive academic inventory will be best positioned to meet these new service realities, as academic libraries provide enhanced services to their faculty and student clientele. More than ever, getting the right book at the right time means getting the right book *fast*. This means that academic vendors must have not only streamlined and efficient buying and ordering mechanisms, but also effective follow-up and claiming methods, and lightning-fast turnaround once a book is received in the warehouse.

Today's academic library also demands a higher degree of accuracy in supply, with less tolerance for the damaged book, the defective book, and the old-fashioned picking or sorting error. Getting the right book, as well as getting the *right* book fast, is the desirable standard which vendors are judged against by their customers.

At Baker & Taylor, the issues of getting the right book and getting the right book fast have been addressed since 1995, when the old internal operating system was discontinued, and a new operating system, the Sales Order Processing system, was installed in conjunction with a new buying system in order to provide the fastest throughput for library and bookstore orders. The new system was also designed to enhance accuracy. Rather than using a traditional method of stowing by publisher, which most academic vendors have used, the system utilizes a random stowing capability. Using radio-frequency technology and a book's EAN Bookland bar code, receivers/stowers scan books into the system as they are received and randomly stowed. Pickers pick titles in waves, and rather than picking titles for an individual library order, will pick multiple copies of the same title at one time, to be sorted into library shipments at the end of the process. All picking also utilizes radio-frequency scanners, insuring that titles are picked accurately; indeed, the system won't let a picker pick an incorrect book. Through use of this system, it is possible for a book to be received, stowed, picked, and sent to a library within an hour. Not only has the system increased timeliness, but also the percentage of errors has been sharply reduced.

With internal receiving, stowing, picking and shipping procedures enhanced, it is just as important to insure that follow-up on outstanding orders to publishers is accomplished with more expediency than vendors had formerly utilized in the past. Although most publishers too have streamlined their operations for greater efficiency in shipping and distribution, and although vendors are sending an increasing number of orders to publishers electronically, thus shortening further the ordering process and enhancing turnaround speed, follow-up on outstanding orders is still a major task for the efficient vendor. At Baker & Taylor, recognizing that the best internal operating system could not operate at peak efficiency unless the books were actually received, an entire unit was added to do nothing but follow-up on publisher outstanding orders. At first, publishers were shocked at the new aggressiveness of follow-up, but they have now come to expect the repeated telephone calls, and are more cooperative than ever in providing accurate updated information on publication status.

VALUE-ADDED SERVICES

Along with increased accuracy and increased speed of service, libraries are also looking for something more from their vendors than they did in the past. Now, all vendors must supply extensive value-added services to be competitive in the marketplace.

Almost all vendors have offered cataloging and processing options. These may include bar coding, theft detection, stamping, MARC records, date due cards and pockets, Mylar jackets, and prebinding services. These had formerly been extremely standardized services, with little customization on the part of the vendor, as libraries utilized their own staffs to conform to localized practices. However, as libraries have themselves been looking for more efficient and cost-effective ways to service clientele and save money, they are turning increasingly to vendors for services once exclusively the domain of the technical services department.

For a vendor to compete in today's market for cataloging and processing, an extensive array of options must be provided. Even the standardized service must offer a wide assortment of options for everything from placement of the bar code to spacing and punctuation of a Library of Congress classification number. This has led to the development of customized library services, where a vendor, in consultation with the library, will provide services which mirror the library's exact current practices. Some libraries are pioneering turning over cataloging, including original cataloging, to the vendor's own professional cataloging staff. Vendors now have many customers utilizing such services; our internal staffs work with libraries to identify specific customer requirements and unique local practices. In some cases, Baker & Taylor is on-line to the library's own catalog, and catalogs with book in hand after reviewing and updating the library's holdings. In essence, vendors are now acting just as another staff member, albeit in a remote location.

In addition to customized services for cataloging and processing, the monograph vendor today must also provide libraries access to OCLC Promptcat service, whereby the vendor transmits invoice manifests to OCLC so that a library's holdings may be updated. Some vendors are also able to receive transmission in return from OCLC so that a label and bar code may be customized for the customer. In this way, when the library receives the book, it is truly shelf ready.

It is not only in the receipt of orders, the throughput, the follow-up, and the value-added services that vendors have seen significant increases in raising the bar of service, but also in the finance area. Campuses are looking for the most efficient ways of doing business with their suppliers, reducing their own costs. This has led to the desire on the part of libraries to charge their purchases to credit cards. The vendor who does not accept credit cards, never a factor in institutional business before, is suddenly at a disadvantage if he does not accept them. For the vendor, there are advantages and disadvantages in the use of credit cards. The biggest advantage is the faster receipt of money, reducing the vendor's days outstanding on an account. Use of credit cards also insures the vendor is paid and significantly reduces the necessity of follow-up by the accounts receivable staff. However, credit cards carry an additional cost for the vendor. Not only must the vendor pay the credit card company a transaction fee on every single purchase, a percentage fee which can range to 5%, but there is, for the vendor, additional paperwork in reconciliation which negates much of the efficiency of the service.

Thus, the monographic vendor finds that in today's environment, the library not only wants electronic ordering, interfacing with its ILS, fast throughput, enhanced accuracy, more effective follow-up, customized value-added services, credit card financial services, it wants all of these services at an increased discount. Vendors are finding that their pencils must be extremely sharp in order to provide both the services libraries desire and an effective gross margin percent in order to be able to develop services such as electronic invoicing, smart bar-coding, etc., even further.

APPROVAL PLANS

It is in the area of Approval Plan services, however, that the bar has been raised the highest during the past ten years. Approval plans first blossomed in the early 1970s, buoyed by large budgets and small staffs, and offering an opportunity to achieve large scale purchasing of core materials with timeliness, better pricing than firm orders, and little front-end work. By the 1990s, approval plans were well ensconced as an effective mechanism for the larger library to acquire current materials, and elaborate procedures existed in most libraries for the review and processing of approval materials. Approval plans had, however, seemed to reach a zenith. Approval plans seemed most practical for libraries with larger budgets. They offered certain disadvantages: an uncertainty of exact dollar expenditures; complex profiling; no interface with firm orders; inability to determine whether or not a title would come on approval; a plethora of bibliographic slips which had to be hand sorted; and no mechanism to predict easily what the effect on coverage would be with profile changes.

The playing field for Approval Plans began to change with the introduction of Yankee Book Peddler's development of Folio, subsequently followed by its GOBI (Global Online Bibliographic Information) system. Blackwell introduced its Collection Manager system to follow its trend setting NTO (New Titles Online), Academic Book Center developed Bookbag, and Baker & Taylor began to develop Aspire (still in development).

What the marketplace now requires is, in essence, more than a mere approval plan. With the development of the Internet, and the capabilities of the World Wide Web, what the marketplace now demands is easy access to a Web-based approval system. Among the desired functionalities of the new Web-based approval plan is the ability to view and edit a profile on-line, eliminating the several weeks formerly required to make changes in a profile. With the profile on-line, librarians and faculty alike can easily determine what subject areas and modifiers are set at slips and what are set at books. It is possible to determine whether titles have been firm ordered or are on standing order, substantially eliminating duplications. Most importantly, a library can determine what has been selected for it in advance of approval shipments, allowing more intelligent firm ordering. Additionally, the capability exists for electronic selection, by both bibliographers and faculty. Slips are a costly business for vendors, both in terms of the costs of paper as well as the costs of postage. The advantages of electronic selection accrue to the vendor as well as the library. Electronic selection allows the library to easily move data between bibliographers, faculty, and the Acquisitions Department, and allows for more individuals to review interdisciplinary titles, in particular.

With the capability to have more intelligent selection, and more upfront selection of core materials, it is inevitable that the approval returns rates will be reduced. Most approval vendors expect between 8-10 percent of approval books to be returned. With the advent of the on-line approval systems, that percentage can easily drop to 2-3 percent returns.

With the development of Promptcat services, and because the approval program captures the core of library materials, many libraries have begun to look at approval programs in a new light. For years, libraries have downloaded approval MARC records for input into their automated systems. It was a small step to go to the next level of approval–receiving materials on the approval program preprocessed, via the utilization of Promptcat for the OCLC update, and vendor processing services for the spine label, bar code, and theft detection. The advantages of on-line selection and the knowledge that the titles that will come on the approval plan are non-duplicative make processing approval program materials possible. Additionally, with a two or three percent return rate, the cost of returning materials becomes almost as much as keeping them, especially when the lower vendor cost of preprocessing materials is factored in.

For the vendor, there are great advantages in shipping materials preprocessed on an approval program. Processing returns from the approval program is an expensive proposition, as reasons for return must be entered and calculated, and extensive credits must be given. When one considers that the eight to ten percent return rate has been the norm for years, one can easily see the extra costs involved considering that most firm order return rates are less than one percent. To scale down approval returns to the barest minimum from a library getting preprocessing has major cost ramifications for the vendor.

One must ask, however, if a library is getting books on the approval program preprocessed, if the program really is an approval program anymore. Instead, what the approval program of the 21st century is becoming is *not* an approval program, but rather an automatic shipment program using a profile-based mechanism to identify those titles appropriate for the library's collection. It is time to develop a new terminology for the new automatic shipment program. If a "slip" is on-line and not tangible, should it still be considered a "slip" or a "form?" Rather, perhaps the new terminology should reflect that of full match to a profile (book), a partial match to a profile (the former "slip" or "form"), and no match at all.

In addition to the trends of on-line profiling/selection and automatic shipment, a new concept for approval plans has been developed with the OhioLink project. In late 1997, academic libraries in OhioLink began to look at the creation of a consortial approval plan. In brief, the concept was for participating libraries to contract with a single approval vendor with the resultant benefits of being able to construct profiles fully cognizant of what other libraries within the consortium had profiled and selected for their approval plans. Through such a plan, libraries could acquire more individual titles and duplicate collections less, thus benefiting all the institutions in the state. Additionally, a side benefit would be that with an extremely high volume of business to one vendor, discounts would be more attractive than if plans were placed with individual vendors. A proposal conference was held in May, 1998, and three vendors were selected to give final presentations–Academic Book Center, Blackwell North America, and Yankee Book Peddler. Yankee became the successful vendor and began to phase in implementation from January 1999.

Certainly, the OhioLink concept will be closely watched to determine if it works as well in practice as it does in theory. Already other states, and other consortia, are beginning to explore the idea of a consortial approval plan since the twin lures of greater discounts and development of more effective, less duplicative collections are powerful enticements, indeed.

The approval plan, once languishing, has had an amazing revival, based on the development of Web databases and the creative thought processes in Ohio. Now, approval plans are in vogue as topics of discussion at conferences, and even smaller libraries and community colleges are beginning to explore the concept of approval programs as viable.

RETROSPECTIVE COLLECTION DEVELOPMENT

In the area of retrospective collection development, the bar has also been raised. With a healthy national economy, and with growth of many campuses and programs, a market for retrospective collection development has emerged, whether for development of new campuses (community colleges, vocational-technical institutions, or even the full-fledged university such as Florida Gulf Coast University or California State University-Monterey), the expansion or introduction of academic programs, or merely extra dollars to be spent at the end of the year. Libraries are turning to vendors to assist them with retrospective collection development instead of poring over catalogs. At Baker & Taylor, the Collection Development unit of Customized Library Services keeps growing as demand escalates. Sophistication in identification of resources is now a basic expectation of the library. No longer is a retrospective list of titles originally treated on the approval program within a certain date range and certain subjects acceptable. Rather, current list production is able not only to consider subject areas, but also to eliminate titles which are out-of-print, to give the exact publication status of the book (i.e., available or out of stock), to state inventory position on the title, to provide academic level and annotations, as well as pertinent bibliographic information, and to do the entire list in hard copy, diskette, or file transfer. Additionally, if a library so desires, its own holdings may be run against the Baker & Taylor database, eliminating in so far as possible any duplication.

VENDOR DATABASES

Perhaps the bar has been raised highest of all in provision of the vendor database on the World Wide Web. Almost all vendors now have some type of vendor database on the Web, available for access, either free or paid, for checking submission of orders. For many vendors, that database consists merely of its approval titles. At Baker & Taylor, the Electronic Business Information Services (EBIS) division has developed TS II, an amazingly powerful search engine on the Web. TS II offers a database of over 2.1 million bibliographic records, including books, spoken word and music audio cassettes and CDs, CD-ROMS, and video, both cassette and laser disc. The database is searchable by a plethora of search criteria, ranging from author, title, keywords, ISBN, LC class, LC subject, approval descriptors, etc., to such esoteric search criteria as movie genre.

For each title, complete bibliographic information is given, including pagination, and even the height and weight of the book. Current publication status is provided (e.g., out of stock, out of print, etc.), and approval modifiers and descriptors are given. Customizable MARC records are downloadable for all titles. What brings particular added value to TS II is the additional information. Jackets have been scanned into the database for all new titles since May 1997. For new titles since 1998, searchable Tables of Contents have been hand keyed, with complete pagination. Additionally, thousands of titles are annotated with annotations from Baker & Taylor publications and other sources. Review sources are cited, including *Choice, Chronicle of Higher Education, Booklist,* and *Library Journal.* For journals such as *HornBook, Kirkus, Sci-Tech Book News, University Press Book News, Foreword,* and a growing additional list, there are full text reviews. Although TS II is a Baker & Taylor product, it is meant to be vendor neutral. One of the highlights of TS II is the listing of available inventory. Currently, inventory levels, both available and on order, are given for all four Baker & Taylor service centers, Koen and Koen-Pacific, and Login Brothers Medical Books. It is anticipated that the number of vendors supplying inventory to TS II will continue to grow.

TS II encourages the building and transfer of carts, which can be detailed by fund or bibliographer. Orders sent through TS II are confirmed, and, if sent to Baker & Taylor, a full confirmation is available within minutes.

TS II raises the bar for both libraries and vendors. For the first time, a library can easily determine inventory levels for a particular title before placing an order. No longer must a library send an order into the void, only to wonder how long it will be before that particular title arrives. Now, a library can determine where a title is in stock and order the title to get it quickly. At that point when the inventory of many vendors is available for view, it will be the vendor who provides the best value-added service post-order–and the best price–who will be the recipient of the order, all things being equal.

The influence of the Web-based database and quick turnaround cannot be underestimated. It is significant that a supplier like Amazon.com has made significant inroads into libraries that have been entranced because of the extent of the database, the ease of ordering, and the apparently quick turnaround. Essentially, a product like TS II gives not only what Amazon.com or Barnesandnoble.com provide, but also more, because it is structured to meet library customs and library requirements.

The impact of the easily public-accessible Web database also requires vendors to improve the quality of their bibliographic data, not only in terms of such basic items as proper spelling and entry, but it also requires the vendor to update status and pricing to reflect the absolutely most accurate and current information. Suddenly vendors are competing not only among themselves but also among entities that did not even exist four years ago.

CONCLUSION

Thus, with the desire of libraries for improved Continuations services and discounts, improved firm order services and discounts, improved Approval program services and discounts, as well as all vendor services Web-based, there has truly been a new service level established. In the new model of service, only the strongest and most innovative vendors with the best pricing and the largest inventory will survive. Libraries will turn ever more to those vendors who can get the right book–and get it in record speed. This will ultimately result in enhanced customer service levels in libraries.

Essentially, what we are seeing is a shift to the information-based vendor. It is not for the purposes of this article to discuss what place the vendor will play in the future, as there is a further transition from the supply of the actual physical monograph to the supply of information. It is clear that certain vendors are already positioning themselves for the next step in the future–Yankee with its Copyright Management division, and Baker & Taylor with its Replica on-demand publishing division. It can only be expected that the bar will continue to be raised further and further, with only the strongest of vendors able to continue to vault.

Content Management for the 21st Century: The Leaders' Role

Susan L. Fales

SUMMARY. This article examines the role of the collection development leader in today's academic library and provides a framework for leadership utilizing the concepts of shared vision and mission, teaching and learning, and stewardship. These concepts are designed to enthuse the seasoned selector, and ensure the appropriate hiring of new selectors, who thrive on change, ambiguity, and constant learning. The leader's role is to provide experiences which teach that content and people are the core work of subject specialists. Content management leadership requires that leaders be exceptional listeners and subject to the same need to continually learn. *[Article copies available for a fee from The Haworth Document Delivery Service: 1-800-342-9678. E-mail address: getinfo@haworthpressinc.com <Website: http://www.haworthpressinc.com>]*

KEYWORDS. Collection development, personnel management

INTRODUCTION

As I thought about the issues of today's library environment, I couldn't help but reflect on my own career of twenty-five years and remember the world that was. Any librarian who has been in the library business for twenty or more years could, and probably would if you asked them, tell stories about the good old days when life was

Susan L. Fales is currently Assistant University Librarian for Collection Development at the Lee Library, Brigham Young University, Provo, UT 84602. Formerly she held positions in the Lee Library as the Collection Development Coordinator, History Librarian, Government Documents Librarian, and Cataloger. She has been an active member of the American Library Association.

© 1999 by The Haworth Press, Inc. All rights reserved.

simpler and the job was in many ways less demanding. Life was relatively unchanging, stable, even comforting in its familiarity and the profession attracted individuals anxious to maintain that stability and comfort. Most librarians were perfectly content to have a virtual monopoly on the knowledge business and saw no need to reach out and market their product. Their contentment was probably quite justified.

The uncharted waters of the "digital library" are anything but comforting. No longer do libraries hold the "collections" that contain all of the knowledge. No longer are librarians the only "knowledge workers" in the business. No longer is it possible to exist as a library and a librarian in solitary scholarly splendor. Libraries have indeed shifted from a passive to an active competitive role in a very fluid business environment.

Harold Billings recently raised an intriguing question: "Are the days of the lone bibliographer or scholar making decisions on their own for the mega-collections as numbered as the lone library making decisions on their own?"[1] It would seem that budgetary and staffing constraints, and technology are moving the profession in an increasingly cooperative model library-to-library and selector-to-selector. What then is the role of the collection manager in today's academic library? Are they even talking about physical collections or primarily intellectual content? How does a library collection management administrator take the staff of yesterday and the staff of today and move the library and its services in the directions that are demanded by the educational and scholarly environment of today and the future?

A BRIEF COLLECTION DEVELOPMENT RETROSPECTIVE

The history of collection development within the academic library has been well documented, especially the developing role of the subject specialist.[2] The shift from selection by faculty members to selection by qualified library subject specialists was an important evolution in academic librarianship. Area studies bibliographers were at the forefront of the move to bring selection into the library, but their success soon led to all, or most, disciplines having collections developed by librarians with, rather than by, faculty. A factor in this evolution was the increasing library collection development budgets of the 1960s. But "fatter" budgets were only the catalyst in the shift. A fundamental reason for the new position of subject specialist or bibliographer was the evident uneven collecting patterns spawned by faculty who had neither time nor inclination to develop balanced collections. Not surprisingly, most faculty were more concerned with their own teaching and research needs, which often resulted in uneven collections in both depth and breadth. A balanced collection needed the oversight of individuals who could look more objectively at the entire discipline and needs of all of the communities supported by the library.

Although there is a forty-year history of subject specialty within the academic library community there hasn't always been agreement as to the role of a bibliographer or subject specialist. The area studies bibliographer of the 1960s was often not a librarian in the traditional sense, holding a subject doctorate rather than a library degree, who chose to express their subject through librarianship rather than teaching. Their role often did not include reference desk work, and resentment coupled with charges of elitism by other academic librarians was not uncommon. Some authors advocated a scholar librarian who needed to be as well versed, or almost as well versed, as the teaching faculty in their disciplines.[3] Others, taking a practical view, advocated a more limited subject knowledge relating to recognition of important authors, publishers, and titles within a discipline, and a basic understanding of the research process, as adequate for collection development.[4]

A model which is quite common today in describing the roles of a subject specialist was hotly debated in a 1968 American Library Association meeting by Robert Haro and Helen Tuttle. Haro recited the functions currently expected of academic subject specialists as collection development and management, library use instruction, reference/research services, faculty liaison, and for many, contributions to the literature of librarianship and their subject discipline. Tuttle took the view that it was an impossible scenario and no one could successfully accomplish the myriad responsibilities.[5] Interestingly, many have accomplished all of these tasks, although certainly with varying degrees of success.

The changes which occurred throughout the 1960s and 1970s to move selection from faculty to librarians wasn't an easy transition. It required a re-examination of purpose and mission. What academic libraries are experiencing today is the same kind of re-examination and another progression in the scope and role of academic librarianship. The implications of today's evolution toward the "digital library" are more visible to our patrons and our institutional administration, and librarian involvement in this transition is no doubt more far reaching than the transition to subject librarianship.

It was the digital revolution of the 1980s and 1990s which moved libraries into a truly cooperative model requiring states and regions, and public and private institutions to work together to acquire digital collections. It also was during this era that the simple life of the lone bibliographer disappeared with the advent of "electronic resource committees" and an incredibly integrative process for the selection, acquisition, cataloging, and dissemination of commercial digital resources. This process is most notably described by Sam Demas.[6] Indeed, subject specialists are beginning to engage in the entire process of re-selection of collections for digital reformatting.[7]

Now as we move inexorably into the 21st century the next stage in the evolution of "collections" and their development is upon us. John Budd and Bart Horloe have borrowed terminology from information science and admirably demonstrated the need to change our thinking and even the words we use to describe what it is librarians do in selecting, organizing, and providing access to information. Their recommendation is that we cease describing ourselves as collection managers or developers, because the word collection implies a discrete physical entity housed in a particular location. In their words, the new bibliographer or subject specialist is a manager of content, moving librarians away from the notion of the packaging of information to its intellectual content.[8] This notion of what we call ourselves and what that "label" means is fundamental in how a leader works with individuals charged with responsibility for the selection of the intellectual content needs of their communities.

THE ROLES OF THE CONTENT MANAGEMENT LEADER

I would not have dreamed as a librarian twenty-five years ago that I would be making this statement, but to paraphrase Shelley Phipps, collection development isn't the key to our future, content management and people are.[9] Content management administrators must strategically frame their leadership work: by establishing a shared vision and a philosophical foundation; by teaching and helping to define the library's current reality; and by paying attention to people, both the content managers and the content consumers or, in other words, by exercising stewardship.[10]

The reality in any organization is that you are working with existing employees, some of whom have been within your library for many years, others fresh from library school, or at least fresh to your library. It will always be a challenge to engage everyone at their various stages of career development and to inspire individuals to make the changes needed in their attitudes, skills, and knowledge base. At no time in our history as academic librarians is it more necessary to make these changes, however.

Organizational and individual learning are the keys to keeping academic libraries in the mainstream of the educational process. Increasingly that innate impulse to learn and to expand our capabilities or to increase our capacities must be built into every organization. By taking the concept of continuous learning into the workplace it is possible to build a vision and mission, to teach, to be a servant leader, and to engage everyone in this process.[11] Senge is completely clear when he states that "organizations learn only through individuals who learn."[12] Not only will the academic library play a dynamic role within the academic community, it will continue to be central to the educational mission if we as content managers and leaders continue to learn.

Shared Vision and Mission

Design is the critical first component for content management leaders. They must involve content managers in the process of defining purpose and mission. In 1994 in the Lee Library, a group of talented subject specialists stepped back from pressing day-to-day responsibilities and spent many hours together exploring their own vision of librarianship, and in those days what we called collection development. They developed the following library mission statement: "The Lee Library mission is the interactive transmission of knowledge to the communities of Brigham Young University."

They then went one step further and identified all of the key words in this brief sentence: *interactive, transmission, knowledge,* and *communities,* and provided a brief list of examples under each word. Under *interactive,* for example, words and phrases such as "mediation between sources of knowledge and seekers of knowledge," "teaching," and "citizenship" were employed. This mission statement transcends physical space and physical collections. It also has the advantage of brevity and memorability. Most importantly the underlying philosophy of content and customer are quietly intertwined with no mention of containerization, cataloging, or even customers. This was a good first step, but we have not yet succeeded in translating the mission into the policies and strategies necessary to move the organization forward at the pace needed.

Although Senge talks about personal and shared vision, he really doesn't provide methods for getting from A to Z in the process. Probably the leading guru of personal and organizational change and growth is Stephen R. Covey, author of the number-one bestseller *The Seven Habits of Highly Effective People: Restoring the Character Ethic*. His philosophy and methodology is actually quite simple, employing the centrality of individual character and principled leadership, coupled with effective relationships, rather than the prominently used quick-fix success literature. As gathered from the title there are seven habits which can move individuals and organizations through tremendous growth.[13]

The second habit, "begin with the end in mind," provides opportunities for greater personal understanding in the creation of a personal mission statement centered on principles rather than social roles.[14] Critical for personal and organizational growth is the idea of first creation, thought and planning, which can then move you to the second creation, the "physical production of desired results."[15] The opportunity to create a personal mission statement and to be involved in creating a library or a content management mission statement teaches the process of visualizing, which increases the ability of the library to accomplish that mission.[16]

The last element of the design leadership is the need to provide experiences and time for effective learning. Leadership is collaborative and no leader can be expected to have all wisdom and knowledge. If it had been left up to me to design the mission statement, based solely upon my own vision, it would have contained a much more traditional direction centering on the selection, acquisition, organization, and preservation of recorded knowledge. Because it was developed through shared vision, it is more powerful organizationally and personally.

Teaching and Learning

Almost simultaneously while the shared vision and mission is being collaboratively developed, the leader must also introduce the process of assessing what Senge calls the "current reality," which stems from our mental models or assumptions.[17] What are the assumptions that we as collection developers (to return to past terminology) might hold regarding collection management:

- Working at the reference desk keeps me informed about what I should be collecting.
- Nothing will ever replace the book.
- Librarians know how to organize information.
- A MARC record is the best way to describe information.
- A PhD will make you a better collection developer. To develop collections subject knowledge must be deep and go beyond the superficial of library knowledge–authors, publishers, format, etc.
- Teaching faculty never really see librarians as partners, but rather second class citizens in the educational process.
- Some librarians are people oriented and others are project orien-ted–effective collection developers are project people.
- Nothing can replace the "lone libraries" individual collection.
- Someone who loves reference work will never make a good collection developer.
- There's no reason to change our titles from collection developers to content managers as our focus has always been content.

Ask any "subject specialist" what the current reality of his library is and their answers would undoubtedly center on the latest crises of the moment–the printers are down, my favorite faculty member just called me to teach his class this afternoon, I've got to take the reference desk this morning because Emily just called in sick or the collection management coordinator insists on having my list of journal titles for cancellation to him by 9:00 tomorrow morning.

The events of the day, described above, are what most leaders and organizations spend their time reacting to. While they must be re-sponded to, it would make more sense to have either analyzed the patterns of behavior (responsive) which would take some pressure off the crisis de jure, or an even more fundamental solution would be to look at the causation of the pattern of behavior. It is this last view of reality which is truly generative and which will bring the greatest learning to our organizations.[18]

Where does the content management leader need to focus her atten-tion within the library? There is no question that at times all levels of learning are taking place but the predominant focus should be on generative learning dealing with underlying causation. You would assume that a library leader had years of professional experience and could anticipate patterns of behavior and their causation and provide assistance, perhaps before a content manager even knew it was required. One way that she could do this is to develop, with the assistance of a team of content managers, a program of staff development in content management which would assess the learning needs of each individual and develop a personalized program to assist that individual to reach the expectations of the organization.

One example of providing structure within the library which can produce systemic changes in thinking will perhaps suffice. One of our humanities specialists was assessing a new Web-based product which would in essence duplicate a print source which in his mind was easier to browse and use. Added to the usability problem was the fact that the digital version did not include all the information found in the print version. As he indicated in an e-mail to me after conducting an initial evaluation, "Mind made up: fun but somewhat superfluous." He went on to say in his e-mail, however, that he attended a meeting on Distance Reference Service, a task force which had recently been established to address issues of concern regarding our mission to the "communities of Brigham Young University." These communities include several institutions of higher education within the United States sponsored by our parent organization The Church of Jesus Christ of Latter-day Saints. He came away from that meeting with an expanded vision that electronic access was mandatory and that in order to serve our off-site customers we had to "make up the difference" in their collections with additional digital content.[19] I could see right in his e-mail a shift in his paradigm from collection development to content management and his personal assessment and adaptation of current reality.

There are also tools which have been developed to assist leaders in working with their staff. I recently had the opportunity to edit a highly collaborative work entitled *Guide for Training Collection Development Librarians* published by the American Library Association. The guide, which was part of the *Collection Management and Development Guides* series, included fourteen modules, each with an introduction, suggested competencies, and sample activities.[20] The sample activities are identified at a basic, intermediate and advanced level. Examples of module titles include Module 2, Planning; Module 3,

Collection Development Policies; Module 4, Selection and Review Process; Module 8, Marketing, Outreach, and Communications with Constituencies; and Module 9, Selector's Knowledge Base.

This guide, coupled with a locally produced content management manual, could provide necessary steps for a new hire, whether a recent library school graduate or just new to the organization, to engage in a career-long learning process. It can set the stage for the library's expectation that learning is always a part of a content manager's work life.

As I was developing individualized learning experiences, using the published guide and our local content management manual, to teach some of our new content managers, I realized that, despite the excellent material contained in both sources, I could not use them quite the way they were put together. The reality was that the guide and the manual are linear in their structure; that is, they move from point A to point Z as though that was the way someone learned all the aspects of managing content and collections. I suppose that it is really the very nature of the printed word and a published book. But because I was trying to instill concepts and overcome the linear problem, I have developed a graphical approach which pulls together various tasks and learning activities from the modules in the printed guide and our local content management manual. Figure 1 is an example of an individualized program to provide training in the "Selection and Review Process." These types of experiences are designed to assist in the individual's continuous learning.

This particular conceptual grouping about the "Selection and Review Process" is a good example of the attention a leader must pay to two types of training needs: the micro and the macro. Micro training relates to "how we do it here" in this library and macro training relates to the larger and deeper understanding of the publishing world, subject knowledge, and the scholarly communication process in specific disciplines. The "Order Submission" and "Other Content Management Policies" both found in the Content Management Manual are micro activities. Certainly Module 4 from the Guide contains both macro and micro concepts. The list of questions found in the guide that a content manager needs to ask while reviewing a book, and which should become second nature in the review process, are certainly macro in their intent. However, the basic level activity in the review

FIGURE 1

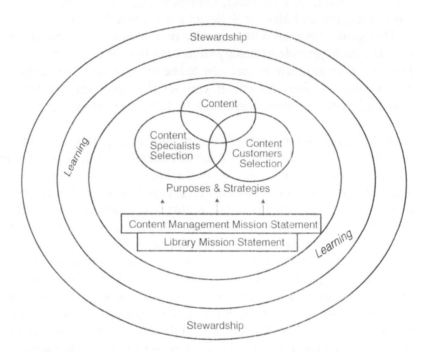

process of "how we review" in this library is undoubtedly a micro level activity. Both are necessary.

Stewardship

On its most elemental level, leaders must care about the people they work with. They must have a desire to serve them rather than have power over them. Management literature talked for years about the idea of management by walking around. In a sense this is leadership by paying attention to everyone, by listening to them, and recognizing them as valuable individuals, not just because they have some knowledge that is needed in the organization. As a part of that listenership, the leader will have numerous opportunities to "walk the talk" by living up to the mission and guiding purposes of the library, and always acting in this consistent manner.[21]

The most fundamental courtesy leaders can give is to truly listen to members of their library. Perhaps in a way the most effective leader in the library really must be the best follower the library has. Stephen R. Covey focuses in Habit 5 on perhaps the most difficult area of leadership: "seek first to understand, then to be understood." Covey describes the process called empathic listening, which goes beyond attentive to a point of engaging both your heart and mind to understand what the intent and the feelings of that person are.[22] These are the individuals out on the front lines selecting the content, teaching the students, visiting with the faculty, and as you think about the process of leadership, there is no question that the people that you work with every day must be listened to or, as a leader, you will stop learning. These are also the individuals who help develop the mission statement and have ownership in the most basic purposes of the library.

There are a number of different ways a leader of content managers can listen, and all of them take time. Leaders, especially if they are more managerially oriented than leadership oriented, are often impatient to get on with new visions and new tasks, thinking they already understand what the needs are at the university. Also leaders often believe that their own personal vision is superior to any vision that a follower might possess.

Recently we established a program of paying attention to people in a fairly formal way by setting up, every other month, an hour-long visit with each content specialist. As a leader I learn so much from each individual, and more importantly I can begin to see where there are both patterns of behavior and even underlying systemic problems which need to be remedied. In addition, for new content specialists there is an opportunity for me to build one-on-one time to teach. Or perhaps to note a pattern of need which would allow me to group individuals who have a common learning need. Certainly as a leader I'm not always the right one to be teaching a particular concept and so it allows others to provide leadership and mentoring and attention to individuals. Assessment of strengths and weaknesses begins to surface in these meetings and strategies for strengthening where it is needed can be implemented. For example, a content specialist might admit a feeling of inadequacy in a particular subject area and a plan could be developed to help them reach an acceptable level of competency in that subject area. The important thing is that the leader as steward is not only strengthening the individual, but also allowing the library to more fully meet the highest expectations as articulated in its mission statement.

Does my schedule always permit me to conduct each of these meetings? No it doesn't, and when a particular content specialist has been missed, it is actually apparent that they feel the need to communicate and be truly heard. I think it is important to emphasize that what is being described here is not a process of listening to everyone's problems and trying to be the arbitrator and solution giver or all-knowing individual in the library. That would consume a leader's time and certainly their energies. One of the most important areas of stewardship is to teach people to think through the issues they are confronted with and to bring solutions to meetings rather than unarticulated problems. If a leader is really leading, then they must insist that no individual meetings of a problem-solving nature will even be held until a clear articulation of the issue is available and several solutions identified, with one solution selected as the best one.[23]

Another important way that the content specialists can be listened to is by providing opportunities for sharing expertise. There is a tremendous amount of staff knowledge that is rarely shared among library colleagues and oddly enough more likely to be shared outside of the library with other colleagues at various library and subject related meetings. We need to do a better job of tapping into the knowledge base of our content specialists. A series of colloquiums where teaching faculty, students, and colleagues could come together to give formal presentations of their research, to share ideas about the changing scholarly communication patterns in their disciplines, and to discuss the dynamic field of librarianship could be implemented.

Recently I had the opportunity of attending an open house for an exhibit that one of our humanities content specialists had selected, arranged, described, and mounted as an exhibit in our special collections on World War I poets. He had also spent countless hours mounting an electronic exhibit which can be found at the Lee Library home page, under *http://www.lib.byu.edu/* entitled "Anthem for Doomed Youth." To watch the excitement of this individual talking with an English faculty member about a particular poet and the differences in the editions of his published works made me realize once again that we need to build into our busy day-to-day lives the opportunities for this sharing of enthusiasm for our subjects and our work. In the highest sense opportunities such as this provide learning experiences for the presenter and the audience, and at the lowest common denominator they have the potential for inspiring those who have taken a less risky path in scholarly research.

Up to this point we have been discussing the stewardship of working with existing people. There is one other dimension that needs to be mentioned and that is the hiring of new content specialists. In the introduction I noted that individuals twenty and twenty-five years ago often entered librarianship because of the comfort afforded in a profession that appeared to change minimally over many years. As is evident, the library profession has not fit that unchanging mold for at least fifteen years. A leader then must recognize that some of the desired employee characteristics of the past will no longer fit the new model employee and take steps to ensure that new hires will suit the new library needs.

It has always seemed important to me that librarians need to be equipped to deal with ambiguity–a world of change. In their article "How to Build a Digital Librarian," Kirk Hastings and Roy Tennant in the November 1996 issue of *D-Lib Magazine* wrote that "digital librarians must thrive on change [and] they should read constantly . . . and experiment endlessly. They need to love learning, be able to self-teach, and be inclined to take risks. And they must have a keen sense of both the potentials and pitfalls of technology."[24] Although their focus was toward librarians who would primarily engage in digital content, rather than the broader-based concept of a content specialist or manager who builds content regardless of format, the characteristics they identified are precisely what is needed today in content specialists or any library position. Within the organization the leader must make it well known that these are the characteristics needed by content specialists in addition to their subject knowledge. How a leader accomplishes this will be unique to their personality and their organizational structure.

SUMMARY AND CONCLUSIONS

The interplay and development of the leader's work, described as designer, teacher, and steward, can perhaps best be seen in a graphic representation. (See Figure 2.) Library leaders can successfully move their organizations into the 21st century–not, however, without growing pains.

FIGURE 2

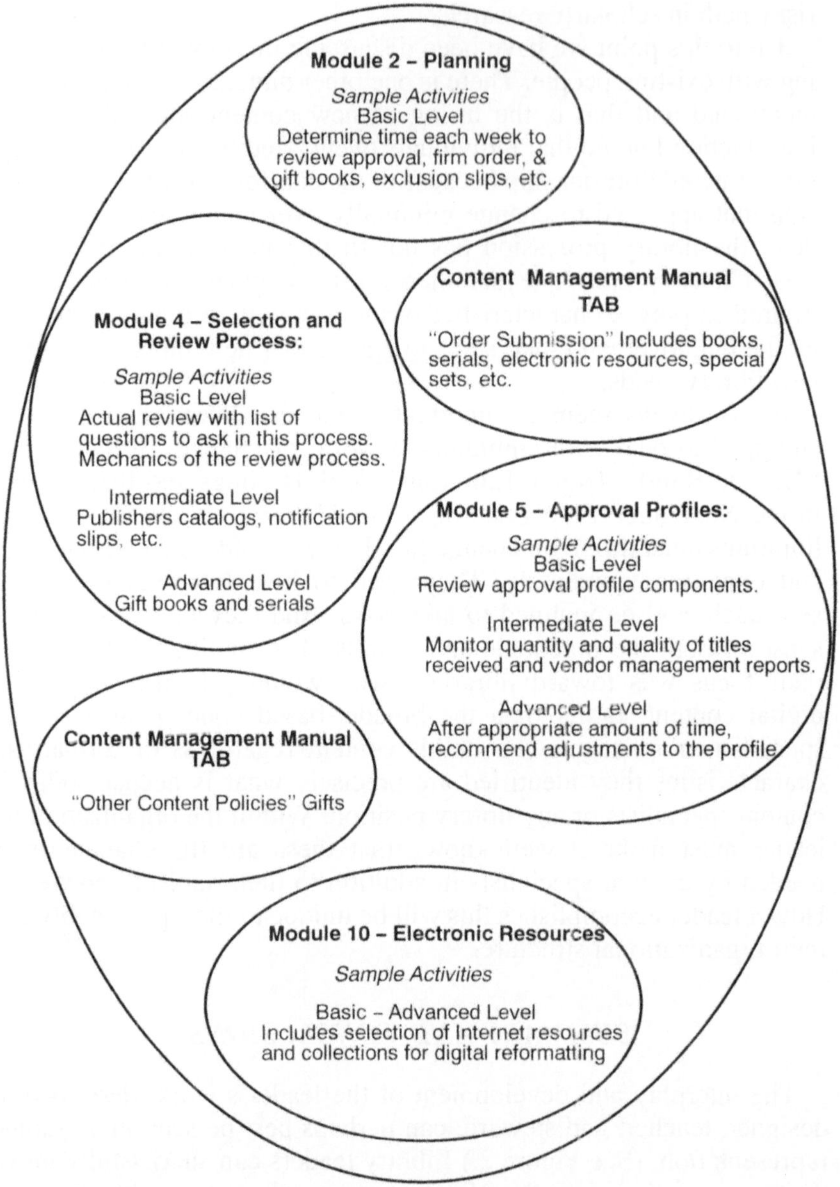

Module 2 – Planning

Sample Activities
Basic Level
Determine time each week to
review approval, firm order, &
gift books, exclusion slips, etc.

**Content Management Manual
TAB**

"Order Submission" Includes books,
serials, electronic resources, special
sets, etc.

**Module 4 – Selection and
Review Process:**

Sample Activities
Basic Level
Actual review with list of
questions to ask in this process.
Mechanics of the review process.

Intermediate Level
Publishers catalogs, notification
slips, etc.

Advanced Level
Gift books and serials

Module 5 – Approval Profiles:

Sample Activities
Basic Level
Review approval profile components.

Intermediate Level
Monitor quantity and quality of titles
received and vendor management reports.

Advanced Level
After appropriate amount of time,
recommend adjustments to the profile.

**Content Management Manual
TAB**

"Other Content Policies" Gifts

Module 10 – Electronic Resources

Sample Activities

Basic – Advanced Level
Includes selection of Internet resources
and collections for digital reformatting

Throughout this brief article, I have attempted to answer the two questions raised in the introduction, but with an emphasis on content rather than collection. What is the role of the content manager in today's academic library? And secondly, how does a library content management administrator take the staff of yesterday and the staff of today and move the library and its services in the directions that are demanded by the educational and scholarly environment of today and the future? I believe that this model for content management leadership, while not unique, will increase the capacities of our content specialists by providing opportunities to learn and grow. The leader's work is to provide both the opportunities and, more specifically, ensure that the library mission, purposes, and strategies are on target. If they do not do this, all the work that content specialists are doing on a daily basis will be for nothing because we as leaders have placed our library's ladder against the wrong wall. Some will say that these concepts seem alarmingly loose in that they do not tie down very specific "ways of doing things." Bearing in mind what Hastings and Tennant described as characteristics for a digital librarian, this content management leadership model must be, and I believe is, adaptable to local circumstances and open to change, and it will move us successfully into the 21st century.

NOTES

1. Harold Billings, "Library Collections and Distance Information: New Models of Collection Development for the 21st Century," *Journal of Library Administration* 24, no. 1/2 (1996): 14.

2. John D. Haskell, Jr., "Subject Bibliographers in Academic Libraries: An Historical and Descriptive Review," 3 *Advances in Library Administration and Organization* (Greenwich, CT: JAI Press, 1984): 73-84; and Fred J. Hay, "The Subject Specialist in the Academic Library: A Review Article," *The Journal of Academic Librarianship* 16 (March 1990): 11-17.

3. Robert P. Haro, "The Bibliographer in the Academic Library," *Library Resources & Technical Services* 13 (Spring 1969):165-174; and John Haar, "Scholar or Librarian? How Academic Libraries' Dualistic Concept of the Bibliographer Affects Recruitment," *Collection Building* 12 no. 1-2 (1993): 18-23.

4. Lynn B. Williams, "Subject Knowledge for Subject Specialists: What the Novice Bibliographer Needs to Know," *Collection Management* 25 3/4 (1991): 31-47.

5. Robert P. Haro, "The Bibliographer in the Academic Library," *Library Resources & Technical Services* 13 (Spring 1969): 163-169; and Helen Welch Tuttle, "An Acquisitionist Looks at Mr. Haro's Bibliographer," 13 (Spring 1969): 170-174.

6. Samuel Demas, "Collection Development for the Electronic Library: A Conceptual and Organizational Model," *Library Hi Tech* 47 (1994): 74-75.

7. The Lee Library recently formed a Digital Reformatting Team (known as DiRT) to establish policy and procedures, similar to those earlier formed at Harvard University and used as the model in the ARL publication by Dan Hazen, Jeffrey Horrell, Jan Merrill-Oldham, *Selecting Research Collections for Digitization* (Washington: Council on Library and Information Resources, 1998).

8. John M. Budd and Bart M. Harloe, "Collection Development and Scholarly Communication in the 21st Century: From Collection Management to Content Management," in *Collection Management for the 21st Century: A Handbook for Librarians* (Westport, CT: Greenwood, 1997): 3-25. I believe this chapter is foundational in shaping thinking and making changes within the academic library community regarding the role of "collections."

9. Shelley Phipps and Cathy Larson, "The Five Disciplines: Learning Organizations and Technological Change," in *Information Imagineering: Meeting at the Interface,* eds. Milton T. Wolf, Pat Ensor, and Mary Augusta Thomas (Chicago: ALA, 1998): 192. Phipps and Larson said "Technology is not the key to our future people are."

10. Peter M. Senge, "The Leader's New Work: Building Learning Organizations," *Sloan Management Review* 32 (Fall 1990): 10-13.

11. Ibid., 7-8

12. Peter M. Senge, *The Fifth Discipline: The Art and Practice of the Learning Organization* (New York: Doubleday, Currency, 1990): 139.

13. Steven R. Covey, *The Seven Habits of Highly Effective People: Restoring the Character Ethic* (New York: Simon & Schuster, 1989, 1990); and Steven R. Covey, *Principle-Centered Leadership* (New York: Simon & Schuster, 1990, 1992).

14. Steven R. Covey, *The Seven Habits of Highly Effective People,* version 2 ([Provo, UT]: Covey Leadership Centre, 1996): 54. Covey lists such social roles as family, work, friend, self, spouse.

15. Ibid., 52.

16. Ibid., 62.

17. Senge, *The Fifth Discipline,* 174-204.

18. Senge, "The Leaders New Work," 11-12; and Senge, *The Fifth Discipline,* 353-357.

19. Robert S. Means, "e-mail," 3 March 1998.

20. Susan L. Fales, ed. *Guide for Training Collection Development Librarians,* Collection Management and Development Guides, no. 8 (Chicago: American Library Association, 1996).

21. Senge, "The Leaders' New Work," 12; and Senge, *The Fifth Discipline,* 345-352.

22. Covey, *The Seven Habits,* version 2, 128.

23. Dale Carnegie, *How to Stop Worrying and Start Living* (New York: Pocket Books, 1944, 1984): 50-53.

24. Kirk Hastings and Roy Tennant, "How to Build a Digital Librarian," *D-Lib Magazine* (November 1996): 2 (http://www.dlib.org/dlib/november96/)

"Uneasy Lies the Head":
Selecting Resources in a Consortial Setting

Gay N. Dannelly

SUMMARY. Selection in a consortial setting is a complex, opportunistic, and often political process requiring an uneasy balance of local needs in conjunction with the group agenda. The issues of the selection and implementation of shared and networked resources, carried out in a comparatively public arena, are discussed in this paper. *[Article copies available for a fee from The Haworth Document Delivery Service: 1-800-342-9678. E-mail address: getinfo@haworthpressinc.com <Website: http://www.haworthpressinc.com>]*

KEYWORDS. Selection management, library consortia, networked resources, resource sharing, cooperative collection development

Libraries today exist in a rapidly changing environment that they neither manage nor significantly influence. While institutional settings differ, the same general conditions exist for all of us and we must identify, evaluate and respond to those environmental forces that most directly influence library services. These include:

* economic conditions;
* technological innovation;
* changes in education at all levels;
* community or institutional priorities and the influences of the environment on local resources;
* local institutional imperatives including changing leadership, financial resources, and changing priorities.

Gay N. Dannelly has been employed at The Ohio State University since 1976. She is currently Assistant Director for Collections.

© 1999 by The Haworth Press, Inc. All rights reserved.

57

Since these conditions permeate our institutions, we must seek new methods to carry out our responsibilities and forge new alliances to retain the centrality of information in an academic setting. One response to these pressures is the rapid development of library consortia as a means to reduce costs and publicly demonstrate efforts to increase services, particularly to students and the broader community.

Library consortia develop for a variety of reasons and in myriad forms. They have been most successful when additional funding is provided to establish shared bibliographic systems, additional online resources, and delivery mechanisms that move materials rapidly from the owning library to the user who requires them. The reasons for and historical development of consortia have been eloquently described in the literature and I will not attempt to duplicate those descriptions in this paper.

In the consortial environment, the selection of resources in all formats begins to shift, allowing for a potentially focused response to use (which is more easily reported from online systems) and to reliance on resources at other institutions. At the same time the traditional academic values require the development of strong, and preferably comprehensive, collections at each local library. While it is clear that no library can meet all the needs of its users, the desire to cling to autonomous self-sufficiency has a remarkably tenacious spirit and the academic library that ignores that value puts itself in peril. However, with time and effort, faculty, in particular, can be brought to see that resource sharing is valuable and will help not only their research agenda, but also that of their students. Without faculty support of resource sharing, the move to cooperative collection development will be slow if not dead.

Consortia have recently concentrated on the acquisition and provision of online resources since those are very visible, can be leveraged by consortial economic strength and size, and are comparatively easily delivered to the desktop of myriad users. Although these programs have significant implications for local campuses and their information technology infrastructures, the positive results of providing online resources are enormous.

Selection of shared resources provided by, or as part of, a consortial effort is as important as selection at the local campus. If a consortia does not demonstrate that it is taking account of the needs of a broad array of users, then the whole effort becomes suspect in the eyes of the faculty, no matter what the student population might feel. It is particularly difficult when such a coalition is composed of either multi-type libraries or libraries of widely disparate sizes. The needs of these libraries might be considered to be quite different and the shared agenda must be carefully developed to be sensitive and responsive to a wide variety of perceived needs. The bases of selection remain the same: authority of the author, subject breadth and depth, treatment level, arrangement, format and any special considerations due to the nature of the material.[1] However, there is now an additional element: visual presentation on the display monitor and effectiveness of the search engine in relation to the content. The values of selection have not changed, but the application of these values is being adapted to both technology and group decision making.

The selection process must be choreographed to show flexibility, broad coverage, some degree of balance in responding to needs and a clear enhancement of local resources. Ideally, it should also allow local campuses to shift their costs to support titles not provided by the consortia. In a recent discussion of five major consortia, Potter notes that while the services provided by the groups are largely additions to existing services, that these have still established new resources for smaller libraries and for distance education.[2] It is also clear that such additions or expansions of services for the local library help to develop a social agenda for the group as a whole, leading to a greater sense of interdependence and a willingness to invest local resources in a larger agenda that will push the group toward an even broader array of services and programs.

Identification, selection and acquisition of specific titles follow varied models depending on the consortia. The Illinois Library Computer Systems Organization (ILCSO) policy " . . . initiatives focus on selecting electronic resources that meet the articulated high-priority needs of its members."[3] Using survey mechanisms, the group identifies high priority titles. Since many of the members also belong to other consortia a high degree of consultation occurs within and between the groups as well as with the participating institutions.

The California State University libraries have focused on a central core of electronic resources that support the common core of the members' curricula, defined as areas offered by at least two-thirds of the CSU campuses.[4] Their review of individual resources uses a specific form to evaluate each resource and includes the results of a hands-on test period. Some results of this process can be viewed online. The reviews are thorough and undoubtedly provide food for thought to vendors whose replies are also provided.[5]

I have had detailed experience with two other consortia that provide very distinct models of selection, acquisition and access that differentiate between those systems with shared hardware and software and those that do not have such a specific advantage.

OhioLINK, a shared state-wide system encompassing more than 70 higher education institutions and funded by the State Board of Regents, provides a shared central catalog, individual library-based systems using the same hardware and software, a library-to-library delivery system, and centrally supported databases and full-text resources. A comparatively mature consortia, OhioLINK uses a system of four library-based committees to develop policies and practices that are then reviewed by a board of library directors.

The selection of resources resides with the Cooperative Information Resources Management Committee (CIRM) with considerable input from the User Services Committee, the group responsible for search engine priorities and applications. CIRM has established a number of subject groups that are expected to generate proposals for specific resources to be made available to the membership. In addition, a strategic plan established in 1994 and regularly reviewed, guides selection of specific resources. Once a specific title is approved, Ohio-LINK staff negotiate with the producer depending on the nature of the content, the method of desired delivery (many of which are mounted on the OhioLINK site under a common search engine), costs, and use restrictions. Members of CIRM may occasionally assist in this process, depending on the circumstances. OhioLINK seeks to use the economic clout of a large, well-funded consortium to get a "best price, best access" agreement. If such an agreement cannot be reached then other resources will be sought to fill the gap in coverage.

While the central funding remains, OhioLINK has now expanded to include two new programs, both funded primarily by the participants. The first of these is a "pay to play" model in which the participants fund a specific resource and only those providing funding have access. The second model, and one which shows the maturity and mutual reliance that has developed amongst the members, is one in which all members contribute to a "war chest" which is used to acquire additional databases for all members. This second model has just been implemented and has been most successful, expanding beyond the initial funding level specified and also expanding the number of databases we have been able to select. This latter model is enabling Ohio-LINK to continue the development of core resources across all major discipline areas.

The Committee on Institutional Cooperation, a coalition of the Big Ten institutions plus the University of Chicago, is an alliance of institutions, not only libraries. With the support of the university administrations, the libraries have sought joint preservation grants, Z39.50 central search engine capabilities for all 13 member on-line catalogs, as well as acquiring electronic resources. All the members are also participants in another consortia, so the balancing act of keeping multiple agendas straight as well as separate negotiating strategies in place is complex. In addition to seeking specific licensed resources, the members, when possible, make their locally produced resources available to other CIC members and one or two members may serve as providers of specific commercial databases for the others.

The CIC selection process depends to some extent on subject selectors who join together to promote a shared agenda that is unlikely to be carried out by the other consortia to which the institutions belong. The CIC "Electronic Resource Officers" (ERO) also generate potential acquisition proposals to the group. The central staff of the CIC Center for Library Initiatives carries out negotiations in cooperation with the EROs to seek the best delivery mechanisms as well as the best pricing and access possible.

In the two cases with which I am most familiar it is clear that while strategic plans and specific preferences in the order of acquisition are in place, opportunism plays a very significant role. This should not be underestimated in any way. It is a significant strategy in and of itself and allows for the libraries, in conjunction with specific providers, to develop major resources that would not otherwise be on the table for discussion, much less acquisition. An unusually good price and good access model will always catch the eye of consortia even if the resource lies outside the expected boundaries of the on-line collection.

Among the most difficult issues facing those who are selecting and providing electronic resources is that of balance: between subjects, formats, costs, and delivery mechanisms. Consortia are perhaps more pressed by the "balance" issue since their constituents come from a variety of institutions with varied and sometimes conflicting agendas.

As a result we, as groups, seek "core" on-line collections and resources. This does provide representation across a wide variety of disciplines and users.

At present, we can't achieve balance by any stretch of the imagination because the resources simply have not yet shifted to electronic presentation in all disciplines. As always, scholarly communication changes differently based on discipline needs. And the formal "printed" channels of such communication change more slowly than those of the day-to-day, scholar-to-scholar discourse. Currently, those publishers who specialize in scientific, medical, technology, economics and business journals are far ahead in digitizing in comparison to those publishers who produce the more traditional humanities and social science titles. The STM publishers have greater financial resources and they have a growing demand for rapid production and provision of information. Publishers of the traditional monograph have just begun to develop new resources in electronic form and again the STM titles are more prevalent than those in other areas.

The strongest presence for humanities and traditional social science journal titles in digital form is found in the serial projects developed by JSTOR and those of the Johns Hopkins University Press Project Muse titles. Both of these initiatives have brought considerable content in the "softer" disciplines to the fore. In addition, a number of publishers have established large full-text collections of materials primarily out of copyright. While there may be disagreements over the editions used, these compilations undoubtedly provide large textual resources for use by humanities students and others who are learning new scholarly techniques of textual analysis which rely on large bodies of text for their application. And they can be delivered to dorm rooms at 3 a.m. for use in term papers!

In fact, it's not clear that we should seek balance in online collections any more than we do in more traditional collections. What we do try to develop, however, is representation. Partially, this is to provide on-line resources across the board to a wide variety of faculty, students, and staff. Even in this approach we are, in nearly all cases, ignoring those disciplines that are either based in, or dependent on, foreign language materials. While some areas, such as Japanese studies, are rich in content, libraries find it very difficult to provide the technological support required for their delivery in the library or even across campus. Specific software applications are necessary; often these are expensive, and require loading on individual machines. Since the users are small in number (although possibly very vocal), such applications are last in priority at most institutions. In other cases, there are few if any digital format materials and the resources used in the discipline remain print based for the present.

In an article supporting faculty, rather than librarian, control of selection of library materials, Dickinson makes a succinct argument for the individuality of collections:

... a widely held assumption (is) that research collections must be "balanced." Quite apart from the lack of any meaningful definition of the term "balance," it is not intuitively clear that a balanced collection is necessarily desirable. With ever-shrinking library budgets, one effect of an attempt to develop a balanced collection will be to distribute increasingly scarce resources over a constant or growing number of subject areas competing for support. The result of this situation, if continued for a sufficient amount of time, will be to produce an "oatmeal" collection, i.e., one which, while perhaps extensive in subject coverage, is uniformly bland, shallow, and undistinguished.[6]

While I would not support total reliance on faculty selection, they certainly must be partners in the process. In fact, the great collections that we all treasure and identify as the most important and valuable at our institutions were built with singular persistence and focus, and probably with an annual battle for funds that might have otherwise been spent on more typical and "average" materials. And I would certainly expect the collection managers with whom I work to continue this tradition!

In our commercial on-line collections we seek to provide representative and core materials. However, the "great" on-line collections are clearly those that go beyond the commercial and attempt to provide digital editions of important and little-held titles and even go beyond that to the provision of manuscripts in digital form. This is both a preservation strategy as well as a way to make primary source materials available to a broad array of users. It's not cheap and it's certainly not easy. But one of the great justifications for such projects is the ease of access for researchers to help determine which collections or items they really must see as opposed to those they can use in a digital surrogate form or eliminate from their research itinerary.

Different scholars continue to need different materials for different reasons. Some disciplines will remain text based, although the form of the text is likely to change as we see digital books becoming more common. Scientists now expect libraries to provide stores of data that were previously the purview of the author. The means as well as the methods of scholarship are shifting to take advantage of the new technologies and libraries must respond to those needs or expect to be marginalized within the near future.

While we seek to find the proper resources for our local institutions as both individual libraries and as consortia, we also try to exploit all the resources that we have and there is no better way of making our presence felt than by joining together with other libraries to develop the strongest possible economic clout. To assist this process a number of guideline documents and sets of principles have been established by specific groups. The use of these documents can help in the negotiation process as well as educating selectors and negotiators about the issues to be faced in both commercial and local project digitizing efforts. Each consortium, of which those described above are only examples, has distinct organizational, political and procedural practices that have evolved as they gain both experience and awareness of local needs. But there are external guidelines that most consortia are now taking into account and that provide additional support and sophistication to the process.

The Association of Research Libraries, in association with the Association of Law Libraries, American Library Association, Association of Academic Health Sciences Libraries, Medical Library Association, and the Special Libraries Association, has established a set of principles for licensing of electronic resources.[7] Additional documents are cited in the Principles that are of considerable assistance in aiding the new negotiator to identify key issues. The University of California system has also developed a separate set of principles that provide a specific view of the realm of purchased online resources.[8] The Committee on Institutional Cooperation, Task Force on the CIC Electronic Collection, which has been working on a variety of issues involved with licensing on-line resources for some time, has prepared a regularly reviewed set of principles.[9]

The latest and most ambitious set of principles has been established by the International Coalition of Library Consortia (ICOLC), a group made up of more than 60 library consortia world wide and rapidly increasing in membership.[10] The rapidity with which such statements have been developed and the pervasive sharing of such documents through various Web sites, most particularly that of the Yale University Library's Liblicense, is remarkable.[11] This site has done a singular service for libraries and librarians as the issues surrounding licensing of electronic resources becomes ever more complex, expensive, and difficult. The rapidity with which the rules of licensing change, as practiced by both information owners and information providers, can be quite bewildering. The Liblicense site provides up-to-date information and alerts for its readers as well as a listserv that also alerts its members to specific problems and allows discussion by librarians, faculty, information owners and publishers.

The process of selection at the individual library becomes one of responding to local need and seeking opportunities to provide access and content at affordable (or at least tolerable) pricing levels. Most libraries participating in consortia are in a constant state of change:

- the library acquires a database locally;
- the consortia decides to negotiate and provide access to the same database;
- the library shifts to the consortial contract for access (which may be in the middle of a local contract);
- the library moves funds from the local to the shared budget;
- the library reallocates for other local resources.

Local imperatives may require that a library make a decision and contract for a specific resource prior to any possible consortial review or consideration, much less negotiation. In the case of OSU, we regularly move from one provider to another as resources are added to those provided through OhioLINK or CIC. While this is certainly not a desirable model, it is realistic and does try to exploit both local and shared budgetary resources to the greatest extent possible.

The library information market is in such a state of flux, in terms of capital investment and commercial cash flow due to shifts in library expenditure priorities, that it is extremely difficult for information providers to establish a standard business plan. Aside from the large international conglomerates, most information providers are seeking new ways to expand or at least maintain their markets. In many cases they are providing information acquisition opportunities of unusual value that generate income based on earlier investments in specific digital resources. Such opportunities tend to shift a library's spending pattern in any single year, as well as shifting the expenditure priorities of consortia. As mentioned previously, consortia are essentially opportunistic organizations and their members are equally strategic in their approaches to providing new resources.

This strategic posture is symptomatic of a new approach in libraries, one that is more akin to the business world, where strategic alliances are regularly established for either short or long term gains and maintained as long as the economic and political results warrant. The result is that libraries tend to acquire as much as possible through the consortial process in order to make the most advantageous use of their financial resources. The consortia thereby takes on the role of the "core" collection in digital format while the local library provides those resources that are very clearly geared to specific institutional needs. These might range from sophisticated technical car repair manuals on-line for a technical college to data resources for a business college to full-text humanities compendia that provide integral textual analysis programs for a university. The diversity that ensues is emblematic of a healthy consortial collection process that seeks to both support the general resources needed at many institutions while also providing the more specialized resources required for very focused or unique programs.

NOTES

1. Gorman and Howes, p. 194-5.
2. Potter, p. 431.
3. Illinois Library Computer Systems Organization, p. 1.
4. California State University Electronic Access to Information Resources (EAR) Committee, 1997.
5. California State University Electronic Access to Information Resources (EAR) Committee, "Database and Vendor Responses."
6. Dickinson, p. 221.
7. "Principles for Licensing Electronic Resources."
8. California State University Electronic Access to Information Resources (EAR) Committee. "Criteria for CSU Electronic Information Resources Core Collection," Jan. 30, 1997.
9. Committee on Institutional Cooperation.
10. International Coalition of Library Consortia (ICOLC).
11. Yale University Library.

REFERENCES

California State University Electronic Access to Information Resources (EAR) Committee. "Proposal to Identify a CSU Electronic Information Resources Core Collection." Sept. 16, 1996. <http://www.co.calstate.edu/irt/seit/elinfo.cc.prop.html.>

California State University Electronic Access to Information Resources (EAR) Committee. "Database Reviews and Vendor Responses." <http://www.co.calstate.edu/irt/seit/ear.rev.fm.hdg.html>

Committee on Institutional Cooperation. Task Force on the CIC Electronic Collection. "Assumptions & Guiding Principles for Near-Term Initiatives." October 19, 1998. http://NTX2.cso.uiuc.edu/cic/cli/licguide.html

Dickinson, Dennis W. "A Rationalist's Critique of Book Selection for Academic Libraries," in Gorman, G.B. and B.R. Howes. *Collection Development for Libraries.* London: Bowker-Saur, 1989, pp. 214-224.

Fussler, Herman H. *Research Libraries and Technology: A Report to the Sloan Foundation,* Chicago: University of Chicago Press, 1973.

Gorman, G.B. and B.R. Howes. *Collection Development for Libraries.* London: Bowker-Saur, 1989.

Illinois Library Computer Systems Organization. "ILCSO Electronic Resources Committee Collection Development Policy." November 6, 1998. <http://www.ilcso.uiuc.edu/web/reports/erc_colldev_policy.html>

International Coalition of Library Consortia (ICOLC). Statement of Current Perspective and Preferred Practices for the Selection and Purchase of Electronic Information. March 1998. <http://www.library.yale.edu/consortia/statement.html>

Kohl, David F. "Resource Sharing in a Changing Ohio Environment." *Library Trends* 45, no. 3 (Winter 1997): 435-447.

Potter, Wiliam Gray. "Recent Trends in Statewide Academic Library Consortia." *Library Trends* 45, no. 3 (Winter 1997): 416-434

Poulos, Angela. "The Best of Both Worlds, " in Gorman, G.B. and B.R. Howes. *Collection Development for Libraries.* London: Bowker-Saur, 1989: 228-231..

Prabha, Chandra and Gay N. Dannelly. Introduction, *Library Trends* 45, no. 3 (Winter 1997): 367-372.

"Principles for Licensing Electronic Resources," July 15, 1997. <http://www.arl.org/scomm/licensing/principles.html>

University of California Libraries, Collection Development Committee. "Principles for Acquiring and Licensing Information in Digital Formats." 22 May 1996. <http://sunsite.berkeley.edu/Info/principles.html>, 22 Oct. 1996.

Yale University Library. "Liblicense: Licensing Digital Information: A Resource for Librarians." http://www.library.yale.edu/~llicense/index.shtml

REFERENCES

1. California State University Electronic Access to Information Resources (EAIR) Task Force, "Proposal to Identify a CSU Electronic Information Resource Core Collection," Sept 11th, 1998. <http://www.co.calstate.edu/irt/eair/eair.html>

2. California State University Electronic Access to Information Resources (EAIR) Task Force, "Reviews and Vendor Resources," <http://www.co.calstate.edu/irt/eair/reviews.html>

3. Committee on Institutional Cooperation Task Force on the CIC Electronic Collection, "Assumptions & Guiding Principles For Electronic Initiatives," October 15, 1998. <http://www.cic.uiuc.edu/faq/egde.html>

4. Dannelly, Gay N., "A Rationale for Criteria of Book Selection for Academic Libraries," in Collection Management and Development: Issues in an Electronic Era, Chicago: American Library Association, 1999, pp. 51–57.

5. Futas, Elizabeth, Library Acquisition Policies and Procedures, 2nd ed., Phoenix: Oryx Press, 1984.

6. Gorman, G.E. and B.R. Howes, Collection Development for Libraries, London: Bowker-Saur, 1990.

7. Johnson, Peggy, "Collection Development Policies and Electronic Information Resources," in Collection Management and Development: Issues in an Electronic Era, Chicago: American Library Association, 1998, pp. 83–104.

8. Joint Task Force on Collection Development Policy, "Electronic Information Resources and Collection Development Policies."

9. Library and Information Technology Association (LITA), "LITA Guidelines for the Selection of General Purpose Microcomputers," March 1998. <http://www.lita.org/committee/techstandards/>

10. Peters, David A., "Resource sharing in an Changing Ohio Environment," Library Trends 45, no. 3 (Winter 1997), pp. 518–530.

11. Potter, William Gray, "Recent Trends in Statewide Academic Library Consortia," Library Trends 45, no. 3 (Winter 1997), pp. 416–434.

12. Taylor, Arlene G., The Tree of Bibliographic Control, Gorman, G.M. and B.R. Howes, Collection Development for Libraries, London: Bowker-Saur, 1990, pp. 228–231.

13. Wortman, William A. Collection Management: Background and Principles, Chicago: American Library Association, 1989.

14. Principles for Licensing Electronic Resources, July 15, 1997. <http://www.arl.org/scomm/licensing/principles.html>

15. University of California Libraries, Collection Development Committee, "Principles for Acquiring and Licensing Information in Digital Formats," 22 May 1996. <http://www.library.ucsb.edu/ucppp/collucla/principles.html>

16. Yale University Library, "Liblicense: Licensing Digital Information: A Resource for Librarians." <http://www.library.yale.edu/~llicense/index.shtml>

Local Information:
Better Utilizing the Data at Hand

Leslie M. Haas

SUMMARY. Today's librarians are expected to be aware of the needs of their patrons, not just at the reference desk, but also in terms of the collection. While there are several articles written about collection development and the many tools available, few address how to take advantage of local resources to develop a patron profile. The purpose of this article is to discuss local collection development tools available to librarians on their college or university campus. *[Article copies available for a fee from The Haworth Document Delivery Service: 1-800-342-9678. E-mail address: getinfo@haworthpressinc.com <Website: http://www.haworthpressinc.com>]*

KEYWORDS. Collection development–tools, collection development–resources, collection development–local issues/aspects, needs analysis, campus resources

INTRODUCTION

The job of the collection development librarian is to allocate the library's limited financial resources in a way that addresses the needs of the patrons it serves. Books, journals, CD-ROMs, and indexes make up a small portion of the types of materials that today's collection development librarians are expected to choose from during the course of a year for a specific subject area. In most college or university libraries, this activity is done in conjunction with other duties

Leslie M. Haas is Head of the General Reference Division at the Marriott Library at the University of Utah. Prior to her job in Utah she was the business librarian at Kent State University and Texas A&M. In those positions she was responsible for collection development and instruction for the College of Business.

© 1999 by The Haworth Press, Inc. All rights reserved.

performed by that librarian. Librarians today are expected to teach classes, develop handouts and bibliographies for specific databases or disciplines, catalog, develop Web pages, work at a public service desk and do collection development for one or more subject areas. Even those hired primarily to be subject bibliographers are expected to do work in other areas of the library. Demands placed on today's librarian demand that we stay current regarding trends in academia and technology in addition to carrying out our daily jobs. We need to be able to look at national trends and determine how they affect the users at our institution.

Who is our audience? How have they changed in the past two years? What areas are of interest to them this year and in the future? These are questions librarians ask themselves on a regular basis. Finding the answers to these questions is not always easy; it almost seems easier to find out about how good a book is versus what changes the Marketing Department is making this year. But, in order to spend the budget wisely, these questions must be answered. The only way to answer them is to use the resources available at the institution.

LITERATURE REVIEW

Methods of gathering information for collection development purposes are widely varied. There have been several articles written in the past few years exploring the ways librarians gather information to help them make informed decisions about the variety of materials they are expected to review and purchase during the course of an academic year. However, the purpose of this article is to examine local resources available to a college or university librarian, and while many articles and books on collection management allude to it, none discuss the types of resources mentioned in-depth. Many of the tools that are mentioned in books are surveys, focus groups, conspectus projects, etc. None really address how to use information produced by departments and other groups on campus and how they may help librarians forming a collection management policy. At the end of this article is a short bibliography of suggested readings for more information on tools available to academic librarians for collection management purposes.

THE ACADEMIC COMMUNITY

In today's academic society one must constantly review assumptions being made about a specific program or college. One of the biggest challenges for collection managers is staying aware of changes made in departments and colleges in response to trends, enrollment figures and changes in technology. Librarians must constantly ask themselves a series of questions. Who are the primary users of a specific collection? Why are they using the collection and what are they using it for? Is the collection of interest to undergraduates? Are faculty and graduate students routinely seeking information on a particular topic? In addition to tools developed by librarians to track usage figures, there are resources on campus that librarians should routinely check to determine departmental directions for a specific program or group of programs. The following section highlights some of the resources available on campus that may be of interest to a librarian writing a collection development policy for a specific subject area.

Every semester professors hand out syllabi to their classes identifying major themes of the class, required texts, reading assignments, projects and a class calendar. Many librarians have found this information useful in identifying trends for undergraduate and graduate circulating collections within the library. Professors are required (as a general rule) to submit their syllabi to the college or department for tracking purposes, and most departments are generally willing to share this information with librarians. In addition to reviewing the texts required for the class, they are also useful to help librarians identify the types of library materials students will need to complete assignments and let professors know if the library can support a specific assignment or project.

Today, more and more professors are taking advantage of technology to place their syllabi on the web. In addition to identifying required readings, many professors also include links to other Web pages that will assist students. An example would be the professor teaching Shakespeare including the Web address to the Folger Shakespeare Library (http://www.folger.edu/). This site includes information on Shakespeare's various works, books about his plays and life, and other tools for the Shakespearean scholar. As students become aware of these sites, they will be returning to the library looking for the books recommended there. While libraries cannot afford to purchase all the books on a given topic, a review of these scholarly sites is useful for selecting books that are pertinent and may have the "stamp of approval" of a well-known scholar in the field. Used with reviews from vendors and other sources, librarians are assured of getting the best product for their money.

In addition to the syllabi, many classes have discussion lists that are established to allow students to continue discussions started in class or ask questions of the professor about an assignment. Depending on the nature of the group, the librarian may ask the professor to encourage students to discuss any problems they had finding the necessary research material for a project. While some of these problems may be a matter of educating the students in the use of the library, the lack of current or relevant material may also be a problem. Using this information and combining it with information from other classes, gaps in the collection that hinder the student doing research can be easily identified.

Departmental Web pages and pamphlets are also good sources of information regarding the research and teaching interests of the faculty. In addition to information on the focus of the program, information about the faculty and staff is routinely included. Many of these pages will discuss a faculty member's curriculum vitae, current research projects and sometimes offer a brief professional biography. The Web pages may provide actual links to a faculty member's vitae. If the departmental Web page does not provide information about faculty research projects, the vitae should provide librarians with a snapshot of the interests of the faculty.

A word of caution is in order here. When reviewing information about a specific program or college, it is important to remember that statistics used to showcase an increase in the number of students enrolled in a program can be deceptive. For example, a graduate program in history may state a growth of 35% over the past two years and not mention that the actual number of students currently enrolled is 30. Another program may show a smaller increase, yet the actual number of students could be significantly higher.

All departments and colleges undergo a review and/or re-accreditation on a regular basis. The departments are required to do a self-analysis prior to the onsite visit of the review team. Many times the library is included in this portion of the process. Librarians may be asked to discuss library use by faculty and students, assess the strengths and weaknesses of the collection, or confirm that the library owns the major scholarly journals in the field and subscribes to the appropriate indexes. The self-analysis also may include a discussion of the direction of the department: research interests of the faculty, plans for future class offerings, new programs, and projected growth rates. These reports can usually be obtained by asking the chair or the dean of the college for a copy, and many times they are kept in the university archives. These reports can especially be useful for librarians new to an area, providing them with direction regarding growth of the collection in specific areas.

In addition to specific academic departments on campus, other departments and centers on campus can provide additional information on the research and teaching interests of the students and faculty. Many campuses have a Center for Teaching Excellence; these centers provide faculty with a place to go to expand their skills in the classroom. Many times these centers will have book clubs, brown bag lunches, and workshops designed to improve the classroom learning experience. Many times reading lists are included to encourage faculty to further develop their skills, and the acquisition of these materials would meet the needs of the faculty and students studying education. Another department on campus that librarians should remain in regular contact with is the research or grants office. As a rule, anyone applying for a grant works closely with this office and they maintain a file of all the grants that someone affiliated with the university has applied for and received. While librarians cannot afford to purchase all the material needed to support a grant, the grant application and description can be used as a way to determine what is currently owned and use the rest of the information to work with the faculty to decide which materials are essential. Also, tracking trends in what faculty are applying for can provide clues as to which way the library's own collection should be growing.

Another important available resource is the university bookstore. The bookstore works closely with faculty to purchase textbooks and other materials for classes. Since faculty are required (or strongly encouraged) to get their lists into the bookstore well before the start of the semester, this gives the library a chance to order books to ensure they arrive as close to the start of a semester as possible. While the bookstore can provide librarians with a valuable list of books requested by faculty, it is also true that many libraries choose not to purchase textbooks because of the expense of replacing them every semester. However, many classes require other material to be read in support of the text chosen for a given class. Many of these books may already be found in the collection, and using these lists can provide yet another way to identify gaps in the collection and note areas that may be of interest to faculty in several different departments. For example, women's studies is an area that is definitely interdisciplinary. It crosses the boundaries of science, humanities and social sciences. If this interest continues and grows, this is a signal to the library to pursue building this collection to meet the needs of the faculty in different colleges and departments.

LIBRARY TOOLS

Local tools refer not just to university and community resources, but also library tools used to identify collection strengths and weaknesses. Departments dealing with access and delivery issues do a very thorough job of tracking titles requested by patrons. For example, in many libraries the ILL Department can produce a report that identifies the books and articles requested by a specific college or department. They can show how many times an article was requested from a specific journal. Circulation patterns change and comparing usage between subject areas shows the areas of interest to different groups of patrons. It is especially interesting to note what type of patron conducts research in specific call numbers. Are they undergraduate or graduate? Used with information gathered from departmental reports, faculty syllabi and other resources, this data can show the library which areas are growing and which are stagnating. And of course another important piece to this puzzle is the question, Why? This should be asked early and often as libraries try to determine how to divide the collection development pie into pieces every fiscal year.

One resource that is helping libraries use their resources more effectively is the library consortium. Today most libraries belong to consortiums made up of either of all academic or public institutions. In some states, these groups are also joining forces to form a statewide network for projects that would benefit users of all types of libraries. The advantage to this networking is the ability to purchase or subscribe to resources that all are interested in, thus decreasing the level of duplication at libraries throughout the state. A disadvantage can be the dilution of Web resources available to patrons. Libraries are encouraged to purchase collections supporting the specialized fields on their campuses and use the consortium purchases to develop those tools that are of interest to a broader group of patrons. While this works most of the time, some universities and colleges rely on the consortium purchases to meet all their electronic research needs.

Consortiums also bring together staff from different libraries to discuss needs at the local level and identify trends affecting all in the specific consortium. Most of these groups work by committee and collection development plays a major role in this network since one of the goals of a consortium is to identify those items of interest to everyone (or a majority). As a result, profiles are developed identifying strengths and weaknesses of everyone's collection, and this can be highly useful for librarians when faced with a major purchasing or weeding project. Most profiles are broken down by subject and identify departmental teaching and research interests, types of degrees offered, budgets, etc.

WEB RESOURCES

While technically not a local resource, the Web is an invaluable tool used by librarians and faculty to stay current in their field. The explosion of Internet technology has made collection management both easier and harder to keep under control. Information comes to us at all angles, and determining what is pertinent to the library's collection is often left up to the individual librarian. The Internet is today's newest way to share research and scholarship with colleagues. There has been an explosion of scholarly materials on the Internet. Sites range from the latest advances in electrical engineering to the latest information on Beethoven. These sites, many affiliated with a known association, collection or school, provide librarians with easy access to information on upcoming conferences, recent releases, available grants, etc. As a source of information today, the Web cannot be ignored.

CONCLUSION

In addition to all the resources mentioned in the previous sections, one more tool librarians must use is the phone or email. It is important to stay in touch with your departmental representatives and key faculty to stay abreast of what is happening and why. Using these tools to communicate regularly with faculty should help a librarian not just stay aware of trends for collection management purposes, but also help them in other aspects of their job.

There are other tools available that librarians can use and it is important to use all those at your disposal in order to make the right decisions for your library's collection. One good discussion group for assisting anyone with a serious interest in collection development should is COLLDV-L. To subscribe, send your request *COLLDV-L@ usc.edu.* The local tools discussed in this article are ones that I have used and were suggested by others who are actively involved in collection management in other libraries throughout the country.

BIBLIOGRAPHY

Buckland, Michael. "What Will Collection Developers Do? Role of Library Collection Developers When Local Collections are Eliminated." *Information Technology and Libraries* 14 (1995): 155-159.

Evans, G. Edward. *Developing Library and Information Center Collections.* 3rd ed. Englewood, CO: Libraries Unlimited, 1995.

Futas, Elizabeth, ed. *Collection Development Policies and Procedures.* 3rd ed. Phoenix, AZ: Oryx Press, 1995.

Heidenwolf, Terese. "Evaluating an Interdisciplinary Research Collection." *Collection Management* 18 (1994): 33-48.

Henderson, William Abbot and William Hubbard and Sonja L. McAbee. "Collection Assessment in Academic Libraries: Institutional Effectiveness in Microcosm." *Library Acquisitions* 17 (1993): 197-201.

Lee, Sul H., ed. *Access, Resource Sharing and Collection Development.* New York: The Haworth Press, Inc., 1996.

Lee, Sul H., ed. *Emerging Patterns of Collection Development in Expanding Resource Sharing, Electronic Information and Network Environment.* New York: The Haworth Press, Inc., 1996.

Nisonger, Thomas E. "The Internet and Collection Management in Academic Libraries: Opportunities and Challenges." In *Collection Management for the 21st Century.* Westport, CT: Greenwood Press, 1997: 29-57.

White, Howard D. *Brief Tests of Collection Strength: A Methodology for All Types of Libraries.* Westport, CT: Greenwood Press, 1995.

Wood, Richard J. "The Conspectus: A Collection Analysis and Development Success." *Library Acquisitions: Practice and Theory* 20 (1996): 429-453.

Zhou, Yuan. "From Smart Guesser to Smart Navigator: Changes in Collection Development for Research Libraries in a Network Environment." *Library Trends* 42 (1994): 648-660.

Serials Management:
Adrift During a Sea Change?

Julie M. Hurd

SUMMARY. Librarians who are responsible for managing large serials collections are challenged not only by changes within libraries and their parent institutions but also by emerging developments in the system of scholarly communication of which libraries are a part. This article identifies some of the significant changes underway within and outside libraries and analyzes their potential impact on research libraries. Issues important to serials managers are explored, and strategies for data-gathering to support management decisions are discussed. Unresolved questions that await future developments or require additional research are outlined. *[Article copies available for a fee from The Haworth Document Delivery Service: 1-800-342-9678. E-mail address: getinfo@haworthpressinc.com <Website: http://www.haworthpressinc.com>]*

KEYWORDS. Serials management, scholarly communication processes, research libraries, decision making, electronic journals/publishing, interdisciplinary research, aggregator services, serials usage, strategic planning, serial archives

INTRODUCTION

Scholarly publishing is undeniably in the midst of a sea change as traditional modes of formal communication are being challenged by digital alternatives deliverable in an increasingly networked environment. These emerging communication formats offer enhanced func-

---

Julie M. Hurd is Science Librarian and Coordinator of Digital Library Planning, University of Illinois at Chicago Library, Box 8198, Chicago, IL 60680 (e-mail: jhurd@uic.edu).

© 1999 by The Haworth Press, Inc. All rights reserved.

tionality over print-based equivalents; some have no traditional counterparts but represent resources or tools not possible in a print-on-paper world. This transformation from print to electronic is especially evident in serial publishing; new electronic journals, as well as electronic versions of traditional journals, are announced with increasing frequency.

Early on, as a few visionaries speculated on the potential of electronic publishing, it seemed that the possibility of decreasing reliance on paper would lead to lower costs for serials. That hope has not been realized. Indeed, electronic products require costly development with demands for technological infrastructure additions and upgraded skill sets among staff, both in publishers' organizations and in libraries. Although few libraries have cut costs by moving to electronic alternatives, many are finding that these products do offer enhanced access and value-added features that users appreciate and, increasingly, come to expect.

At the same time as libraries are faced with escalating costs for serials, other changes within our larger environment present new demands and offer new challenges. Whether the changing environment of research and higher education, or the emergence of new communication paradigms, the implications are present for library managers who are asked to add new resources, develop new services, and reach new patron groups, all with only modest budget increases to offset inflation and to launch new initiatives.

SOCIETAL AND ORGANIZATIONAL CHANGE AGENTS

Two developments impacting research libraries are sweeping societal changes:

- "Bigger Science" and the growth in interdisciplinary research
- The Internet and the World Wide Web

Historian of science Derek Price wrote of "Big Science," his term for post-World War II scientific research that was characterized by large-scale, often government-funded, team projects such as the construction of high energy physics research facilities or the launching of health care initiatives directed toward discovering cures for diseases such as cancer. I use the term "Bigger Science" to emphasize that we have moved even further along a growth curve toward multi-national, interdisciplinary initiatives with global significance in efforts such as the manned space station, the International Thermonuclear Experimental Reactor, the Hubble Space Telescope, and the Compton Gamma Ray Observatory. "Bigger Science" projects have increased the sense of immediacy among participants; without computer-mediated communication and real-time data-sharing the projects would not be possible. "Bigger Science" has also contributed to the growth of the journal literature. In the life sciences the genome databanks that are being built collaboratively provide repositories of validated genetic sequencing data that can be accessed by any scientists who are connected to the Internet. The Internet and the World Wide Web support globalization and rapid communication of research results, whether raw data, preliminary analyses, or completed reports.

Concurrent with the growth of networked communications, digital libraries are emerging that promise to eliminate geographic constraints for information seekers. Powerful desktop computers connected to the Internet are reducing the need to frequently visit library facilities as the scholar's workstation becomes a reality. Studies of information seeking document that researchers, particularly in the sciences, are adopting information technologies and changing their work habits to reflect an increasingly networked electronic environment. John Walsh and Todd Bayma (1996) have studied the impact of computer-mediated communication on scientific work; they identified discipline-dependent variations in the adoption of technology and explain these differences in terms of the different social structures and organizational contexts of each field. Lisa Covi and Rob Kling (1996) focused on the organizational and behavioral aspects of creation, promotion, and use of digital libraries by faculty, librarians, and computer support providers in a research university environment. Covi and Kling found that faculty use of digital library resources was related to the value system of their invisible college. The models they proposed offer a framework for a better understanding of effective design and use of electronic resources.

Walsh, Bayma, Covi and Kling were among the first to document adoption of information technology by scholars. Their publications provide a snapshot early in a transition from a primarily print-based environment to one that is increasingly digital. The work habits of future scholars that might be imagined by extrapolating their findings will certainly be more dependent on workstations and networks. Whether they rely on preprint databases, search with Web-based finding tools, or read electronic journals, scholars are coming to expect that their libraries will provide access to state-of-the-art electronic resources to support their research.

NEW COMMUNICATION AND PUBLISHING PARADIGMS

Computer technology has also contributed to the development of new communication and publishing paradigms. The earliest applications of computers in scholarly publishing were in typesetting, and these provided dramatic reductions in the time from acceptance of a manuscript to appearance of a publication in print. Secondary service publishers who produced indexes and abstracts to the journal literature benefited during the 1960s from National Science Foundation grants that provided them with seed funding to employ technology to produce more timely indexes. A natural by-product was the development of bibliographic databases that today are the preferred mode for literature searching in many disciplines. More recently the primary literature of scholarship, the journal, has begun a migration to a digital format. It may be too soon to assess the impact of electronic journals on information-seeking behavior, but a recent analysis of information-seeking patterns by Carol Tenopir and Donald W. King (1998) has measured growth in the use of electronic resources. They predict that, to the extent that electronic publishing facilitates browsing and automated searching, it will be used by growing numbers of readers.

Electronic journals have made feasible new distribution models for information such as the development of aggregator services. While document delivery services based on mailed copies of individual articles existed prior to the emergence of electronic journals, it is the availability of their digitized contents that now allows an information-seeker to review an article on the desktop workstation and, with a very few keystrokes, download the entire article for storage or printing. Business models and licensing agreements designed to protect publishers' revenue streams are developing to accommodate this mode of delivery; some of these models appear to offer potential cost savings to libraries as well.

The use of familiar bibliographic databases linked to source electronic journals is a logical development in the delivery of information using the article as the unit of distribution. Libraries are asking whether it makes good sense to consume some journals "by the glass" and to subsidize the ordering of copies of articles when requested by users. Gary W. White and Gregory A. Crawford (1998) employed a cost-benefit analysis to explore whether subscribing to a full-text database that allowed users to obtain articles from journals not held by the library was preferred over use of traditional interlibrary loan. They examined both potential cost savings and benefits to the library and concluded that, while expenses may not be reduced when such a new service is implemented, users do benefit. White and Crawford acknowledged that, while the full-text database might have higher direct costs over interlibrary loan, users received added value from the database including immediate access to needed information. The library also saved staff time that would have been used to process interlibrary loan requests. Their methodology and the thoughtful analysis of additional relevant factors provides a model that other libraries may find instructive.

Another distribution model currently in test stages is represented by Elsevier Science's PEAK (Pricing Electronic Access to Knowledge) experiment (1998). The PEAK project, in which Elsevier is collaborating with the University of Michigan and other libraries, is an experiment to investigate new approaches to packaging and pricing digital information. PEAK offers participants access on Michigan's host server to 1200 Elsevier Science journals through several pricing models. One of these is an innovation they have called a "generalized subscription" which allows users at a participating library to select a predetermined number of articles from among those in the entire database of articles. Once selected, an article becomes part of an institution's "holdings" in a digital library; no further charges are incurred for subsequent uses of that article. This experiment is scheduled to run through mid-1999 and seem likely to play an important role in the development of Elsevier's business models for pricing electronic information.

AGGREGATOR SERVICES

The emergence of aggregator services represents a different approach to information delivery based on electronic subscriptions. In the aggregator model a library purchases access to a selection of electronic journals; the aggregator serves as a front-end and gateway to journal content by providing a search engine and links to the articles identified during a search. Some aggregators are subscription agencies such as Blackwell, Dawson, or EBSCO who have identified a new service role for themselves in an electronic environment. Typically, the aggregator has entered into partnerships with publishers and connects a user to a chosen article on the publisher's server after appropriate validation of his/her right to access the journal. Aggregators can provide added value to a library by offering a common search engine for a large number of titles to which a library subscribes, by assisting in negotiating licensing agreements, and by providing an electronic archive. Users appear to enjoy the seamless interface that eliminates intervening steps involving library journal lists or catalogs and the introductory publisher and journal title screens they would see if they went directly to a publisher site through a Web catalog link. At present many aggregators assess charges on a per title basis. Since a large research library may decide to use multiple aggregators, the library may be adding costs that reflect overlap in title coverage by services. Sorting out when paying for overlap makes sense is a new challenge faced by fund managers.

Malcolm Getz (1997) has examined the economics of electronic publishing and has analyzed some of the emerging distribution schemes in detail. Getz sees advantages for libraries in the packaging of large numbers of electronic journals into a single database representing a single purchase, somewhat in parallel to the use of subscription agencies to handle large numbers of paper subscriptions. In the shift to electronic publication he sees increased value in the database as the unit of distribution for research libraries. A possible outcome he projects involves easier exploitation for profit by publishers and, potentially, a negative impact for library budgets. California State University clearly has recognized the values added by aggregators but is taking a proactive approach by putting out its own RFP for a customized aggregation of e-journals as reported by Lisa Guernsey (1998). Rather than choosing from among available collections assembled by aggregators, the 23-campus university has identified over 1,250 titles it wants. It is willing to pay any provider who can meet the university's needs by building the database the campuses want. As this was written it was too early to know the outcome of this approach; it certainly will bear watching.

Electronic publishing is very dynamic and will likely remain so for some time to come. Although some publishers, such as Elsevier, are experimenting with new delivery and pricing models many others are concerned about maintaining their revenue streams and are adopting conservative business models that typically require print subscriptions in order to purchase electronic access. A few publishers, such as Academic Press, offer packages in which a subscriber to many Academic print titles can gain access to additional Academic electronic titles not held in print form. At present electronic subscriptions without corresponding print subscriptions are not available for all titles.

CLIMATE OF CHANGE

We are in the midst of a transition from print to electronic information. While the future is not fully imaginable, the transformation in process has already dispelled some of our earliest hopes that lower costs for serials would follow from paperless publication. The emerging models of delivery will likely lead to new partnerships and alliances among scholars, publishers, libraries, and scholarly associations; the discussion above identified examples of these. We may expect to see choices in packaging of information ranging from the "pay-per-look" article-level option through the large aggregator-compiled database of multiple electronic journals with value-added features provided by links to related information. To make informed choices from an increased array of products libraries will require an in-depth understanding of their own users' needs evaluated in the context of their institutional mission and goals. The next section in this article will address strategies for library decision-makers and suggest approaches for data-gathering in support of serials management.

STRATEGIC PLANNING FOR SERIALS DECISIONS

At present, most serials decisions are made on a title-by-title basis grounded in an understanding of the detailed information needs of a library's primary user community. For university libraries, this group consists of faculty, staff, and students. Librarians developing a serials collection rely on historic data on what has been requested and used and, at the same time, try to anticipate future needs. We assume that recent past uses of a collection will predict significant portions of the future need. Strategies suited to

answering detailed questions about library use include both unobtrusive and obtrusive methodologies.

Unobtrusive measures of use of a serials collection include those
approaches that rely on data gathered without direct interaction with
information seekers:

- circulation data
- in-house use studies
- citation analyses.

Obtrusive measures rely on surveys, interviews, and observations
of information seekers. The two types of data gathering are complementary and may be used in tandem to obtain a more complete picture
of collection use. Nancy J. Butkovich (1996) has reviewed published
use studies that employed both obtrusive and unobtrusive measures to
assess collection use.

UNOBTRUSIVE MEASURES OF SERIALS USAGE

Circulation statistics are routinely collected by most libraries; analyzed reports are a feature of most automated circulation systems now
available. If a library's journal collection circulates, teasing out statistics on journal use from all circulation statistics is generally possible.
These data, however, tend to reflect only part of the use of a journal
collection; much more use is likely to be in-house as users read and
photocopy articles of interest without ever checking out materials. Of
course, this fact is well-known to collection managers who have developed measures of in-house usage such as reshelving studies that
collect data from materials left by patrons to be reshelved. If materials
are located in closed stacks or off-site storage facilities, requests from
users provide still other sources of data. The combination of circulation statistics and in-house use data together offer insights into specific
titles as well as into the ages of print materials consulted most.

As increasing numbers of journals are acquired in electronic form,
it will be even more important to obtain detailed usage data to justify
what will likely be increased serials costs. Electronic publishers and
aggregator services will certainly be collecting this data for their own
use as they attempt to develop economically viable digital products.
Serials managers will need to be vocal in articulating their needs as

well; provision of regular and meaningful usage reports for customers should be included in contract negotiations for electronic products.

Data on journal use collected from circulation systems, in-house use studies, and reports from vendors of electronic products provide information on titles used by all library patrons. Citation analyses allow a focus on the usage by those patrons engaged in research and publication, certainly a primary constituency for research libraries. Citation analyses may explore documented use of materials by scholars in an entire field or specialization; there are numerous such reports in the professional literature and these are useful to serials managers for the discipline-wide perspective they offer. For example, the Institute for Scientific Information (ISI) publishes *Journal Citation Reports* that can be used to rank, evaluate, categorize and compare journals. Their coverage is interdisciplinary and international and includes journals from over 3,000 publishers from 60 countries. (*Journal Citation Reports.* Philadelphia, PA: Institute for Scientific Information, annual. Separate compilations for science/technology and social sciences.) The *Journal Citation Reports* are valued by individual scholars, university promotion and tenure committees, and library managers for the insights they offer on scholarly journals.

A journal-based citation analysis by Stephen Harter (1996) provides some of the first data on citations to electronic journals. Harter has documented the contributions of the first electronic journals to scholarly communication by tracking citations to articles that appeared in 39 scholarly electronic journals that began publication no later than 1993. His citation-based measures of impact provide baseline data that can be augmented by additional studies of this emerging format.

Another innovation is the electronic preprint ("e-print"), a phenomenon characteristic to physics, astronomy, and mathematics literatures. E-prints represent a mode of distribution at the article level that spans the boundary between informal and formal communication. Physicist Paul Ginsparg has been a leader in developing the e-print; his e-print server at Los Alamos National Laboratory (http://xxx.lanl.gov) was described in an article in *Computers in Physics* (1994). Gregory K. Youngen (1998) has measured the growing importance of e-prints through a citation analysis using the ISI SciSearch database. He also discusses issues related to the future role of e-prints in scientific communication including linking e-prints to published articles that supersede them, maintaining the integrity of e-print servers, and archival concerns.

Another type of citation analysis that focuses on a local population of researchers provides complementary information on journal use to that found in *Journal Citation Reports* or in discipline-wide or journal-based citation analyses. Cited here are studies of local populations of biologists; comparable studies exist for populations in other disciplines, primarily in the sciences. An early "local citation analysis" was conducted by Katherine W. McCain and James E. Bobick (1981) who examined citations in faculty publications, doctoral dissertations, and preliminary doctoral qualifying briefs to assess journal use by the biology department at Temple University. Rosalind Walcott (1994) obtained "local knowledge" concerning users of the biology library at the State University of New York at Stony Brook by analyzing citation patterns in theses and dissertations. Walcott used her findings to support a serials cancellation project and other collection development and management decisions. Janet Hughes (1995) utilized faculty publications from Pennsylvania State University coupled with *Journal Citation Reports* data to create a ranked list of serials in molecular and cellular biology for a serials evaluation project. She discovered interdisciplinary citation patterns as well as usage that identified specializations among her constituency. This author, working with colleagues Deborah D. Blecic and Rama Vishwanatham, analyzed journal use by molecular biologists at the University of Illinois at Chicago (1999). Our derived list of core journals in molecular biology shares titles with Walcott's and Hughes' lists but also includes unique titles. Variations among the three populations likely reflect research specializations on the three campuses and argue for the value of "local citation analyses" to support institutional decisions.

OBTRUSIVE MEASURES OF SERIALS USAGE

Questionnaires, surveys, and interviews also provide serials managers with information to support decision-making. Asking users about journals may be accomplished systematically through a survey instrument or a structured interview or, less formally, in meetings with faculty or one-on-one discussions. Butkovich identifies studies of this type in her 1996 review article cited earlier. Systematic techniques, borrowed from the social sciences, also may be used to assess whether users will be receptive to innovations such as electronic journals or new modes of information delivery. Tenopir and King's 1998 study of e-journals is an example of such research.

UNANSWERED QUESTIONS AND UNRESOLVED ISSUES

The strategies for data gathering described above draw on the recent past and the present to inform serials decisions. The sea change we are experiencing may give rise to new questions we have not thought to ask and for which we have no reliable source of data. Our decisions may be affected by factors outside our immediate sphere of influence that are behavioral, economic, or legal in nature.

We are beginning to see how the impact of technology on scholarly communication is causing changes in the information-seeking behavior of researchers. Simultaneously economic considerations are giving rise to new forms of packaging and new modes of delivery of information that come with licensing constraints unlike those in the print-on-paper past. The future will likely evolve from developments such as these.

What innovations bear watching because they will impact serials management? Communication models that have potential to diminish the role of the scholarly journal have been proposed by some; whether these will provide the element of peer review so important in scholarly reward systems may influence their adoption. Altered roles for associations, publishers, and other producers and distributors of journal-based information are giving rise to new business models and organizational missions. Which of these will prove viable we shall learn in time.

ARCHIVAL CONCERNS

Many institutions are currently subscribing to both print and electronic versions of journals. While electronic copy without print is not always an option, a compelling argument for this "duplication" is that of enhancing research productivity by providing desktop access to key resources while retaining a paper archive for future use. At the present time little has been done to assure access to growing backfiles of electronic journals. This is an area of rapid development with several promising directions emerging:

- Professional association publishers such as the American Astronomical Society are proposing to serve as the archive for their own electronic publications. Whether commercial publishers will offer comparable archives for their publications is an unanswered question.
- University-based electronic archives are also possible. This parallels the paper archival collections held by research libraries. The desirability of this has been best argued in a 1996 report to the Commission on Preservation and Access and the Research Libraries Group, *Preserving Digital Information: Report of the Task Force on Archiving of Digital Information.*
- Ovid Technologies, Inc., a commercial provider of full-text electronic journals in science, technology, and medicine, has announced an electronic archive policy designed to address customers' concerns related to ownership and archiving. Working with primary publishers Ovid has outlined strategies based on archival CD-ROM distribution coupled with access to publishers' Web archives.

These initiatives offer encouragement to those responsible for assuring ongoing access to scholarly information; any or all of these could shape a digital archive.

The uncertainties induced by change will likely continue for the immediate future. This article has attempted to identify some key determinants and to suggest data that might inform strategic planning by serials managers. The insights offered here represent informed speculation based on observation. That serials managers will monitor all these initiatives, and others not yet underway, is part of the challenge that comes with their responsibilities.

REFERENCES

Butkovich, Nancy J. "Use Studies: A Selective Review." *Library Resources & Technical Services* 40, no. 4 (October 1996): 359-368.

Covi, Lisa and Kling, Rob. "Organizational Dimensions of Effective Digital Library Use: Closed Rational and Open Systems Models." *Journal of the American Society for Information Science* 47, no. 9 (1996): 672-689.

"Elsevier Science and the Digital Library." http://www.elsevier.nl/cgi-bin/inca/esavshownews?item-OTH/1998-Q3/serval.elsevier.n111253 (1998).

Getz, Malcolm. "An Economic Perspective on E-Publishing in Academia." *Journal of Electronic Publishing* 3, no. 1 (September 1997). http://www.press.umich.edu/jep/archive/getz.html

Ginsparg, Paul. "First Steps toward Electronic Research Communication." *Computers in Physics* 8, no. 4 (July/August 1994): 390-396.

Guernsey, Lisa. "In a Turnabout, California State U. Calls for Bids from Data-Base Companies." *The Chronicle of Higher Education* (1988). http://chronicle.com//daily/98/12/98121801t.htm

Harter, Stephen P. "The Impact of Electronic Journals on Scholarly Communication: A Citation Analysis." *The Public Access Computer Systems Review* 7, no. 5 (1996): 5-34. http://info.lib.uh.edu/pr/v7/n5/hart7n5.html

Hughes, Janet. "Use of Faculty Publication Lists and ISI Citation Data to Identify a Core List of Journals with Local Importance." *Library Acquisitions: Practice & Theory* 19, no. 4 (1995): 403-413.

Hurd, Julie M., Blecic, Deborah D. and Vishwanatham, Rama. "Information Use by Molecular Biologists: Implications for Library Collections and Services." *College & Research Libraries* 60, no. 1 (January 1999): 31-44.

McCain, Katherine W. and Bobick, James E. "Patterns of Journal Use in a Departmental Library." *Journal of the American Society for Information Science* 32 (July 1981): 256-261.

Preserving Digital Information: Report of the Task Force on Archiving of Digital Information. Washington, DC: Commission on Preservation and Access and The Research Libraries Group, Inc., 1996.

Tenopir, Carol and King, Donald W. "Designing Electronic Journals with 30 Years of Lessons from Print." *Journal of Electronic Publishing* 4, no. 2 (December 1998). http://www.press.umich.edu/jep/04-02/king.html

Walcott, Rosalind. "Local Citation Studies–A Shortcut to Local Knowledge." *Science & Technology Libraries* 14, no. 3 (1994): 1-14.

Walsh, John P. and Bayma, Todd. "Computer Studies and Scientific Work." *Social Studies of Science* 26, no. 3 (1996): 661-703.

Walsh, John P. and Bayma, Todd. "The Virtual College: Computer-Mediated Communication and Scientific Work." *The Information Society* 9 (1996): 343-363.

White, Gary W. and Gregory A. Crawford. "Cost-Benefit Analysis of Electronic Information: A Case Study." *College & Research Libraries* 59, no. 6 (1998): 503-510.

Youngen, Gregory K. "Citation Patterns to Traditional and Electronic Preprints in the Published Literature." *College & Research Libraries* 59, no. 5 (1998): 448-456.

Index

© 1999 by The Haworth Press, Inc. All rights reserved.

*For Product Safety Concerns and Information please contact
our EU representative GPSR@taylorandfrancis.com Taylor & Francis
Verlag GmbH, Kaufingerstraße 24, 80331 München, Germany*

T - #0153 - 270225 - C0 - 212/152/6 - PB - 9780789010032 - Gloss Lamination